CRUEL AND
UNUSUAL PUNS

Accidental slips of the tongue and intentional transpositions can turn song and book titles, famous quotations, and familiar proverbs into naughty—or nice—ticklers of the funny bone. They also make this book of classic and original Spoonerisms a punster's delight.

As the madam said at the S&M party, it's bound to be fun (and fun to be bound)! So even if life can't be all *Runelight and Moses* (a new musical inspired by the Ten Commandments), there are more laughs here than you can stake a Schick at!

This hilarious encyclopedia of Spoonerisms is sure to lift your spirits (or, if you work out with weights, spirit your lifts). Don't heave loam without it!

Have you heard the ones about . . .

The inner-city video game called *Super Barrio Mothers*? The new self-help book on postpartum depression, *The Blues of the Birth*? The horror film *She Conks to Stupor*? Or the TV series about the psychiatrist whose patients are comedians: *Honey, I Kid the Shrink!*

No?

Well, this wacky, wonderful volume of topsy-turvy humor will brighten your day and elevate your intellect . . . all while it encourages you, as a Dutch plumber might suggest, to "go thou and loo dikewise."

Cruel and Unusual Puns

"This definitive treasury of transposition puns is truly a re-wording experience. Many of Hauptman's clever reversals might be called *forkerisms*—spoonerisms with a point. And the point is the marvelous tricks that we human beings are capable of playing with the English language."

—Richard Lederer, author of *Anguished English* and *Get Thee to a Punnery*

CRUEL
AND
UNUSUAL PUNS

Don Hauptman

Illustrations by Arnie Levin

LAUREL

A LAUREL BOOK
Published by
Dell Publishing
a division of
Bantam Doubleday Dell Publishing Group, Inc.
666 Fifth Avenue
New York, New York 10103

ISBN: 0-440-20850-5

Printed in the United States of America

Published simultaneously in Canada

December 1991

10   9   8   7   6   5   4   3   2   1

OPM

Acknowledgments

Many people assisted in my research, contributing puns, documents, citations, translations, suggestions, and insights. In compiling the following list, I've probably overlooked someone. You know who you are, and when you tell me, will my race be fed!

—D.H.

Dr. Frank Abate, Dr. Isaac Asimov, Bob Bly, Reginald Bretnor, Dan Carlinsky, Fred Cookinham, John Crosbie, Ed Crosby, A. Ross Eckler and Susan Eckler, Louise and Willard R. Espy, Barry Farber, Prof. Victoria A. Fromkin, Lewis Burke Frumkes, Eugene Gramm, Gerhard Gschwandtner, Mary Hauptman, Dr. Robert Hauptman, Julie Holtzman, Harold Holzer, Dave Kahn, Michelle Kamhi, David Kennedy, Robert D. Kephart, Frieda Leibler, Dr. E. James Lieberman, Sharon Lowenheim, Richard Markowitz, Curt Monash, Prof. Don L. F. Nilsen, Jeffrey Norton, Dyanne Petersen, Milt Pierce, Dr. Hans Rollmann, Rob Schleifer, Robert A. Steiner, Richard Stoddard, Mark Tier, Laurence Urdang, Bernard Wastin, Earl Wrightson, Cathy Young.

Also . . .

Mary Ann Madden, editor of The *New York* Magazine Competition, and Lenore Skenazy, editor of "T.N.T./The Next Trend" in *Advertising Age,* in whose amusing columns some of my compositions originally appeared.

Jackie Cantor and Leslie Schnur, my editors at Dell, and Alfred P. Lowman and B. G. Dilworth, my literary agents.

My parents, Sigrid and Irving Hauptman, both teachers, who imparted to me from an early age an appreciation for the pleasures of language and word-play.

And especially fellow Intrepid Linguist Richard Lederer, an unflagging source of inspiration, encouragement, and valuable advice.

Dedication

To a man who was the faster of his mate:
The Reverend Dr. William Archibald Spooner
(1930–1844)
Without whom this book would not be possible . . .
or even necessary.

CRUEL
AND
UNUSUAL PUNS

Cable of Tontents:

INTRODUCTION
Silver Spoonerisms

(Including "The Official Rules")

Have you heard about the inner-city video game called *Super Barrio Mothers*? The musical version of *The Ten Commandments,* to be titled *Runelight and Moses*? Or that new self-help book on postpartum depression, *The Blues of the Birth*?

Welcome to the wonderful world of *spoonerisms*—also known as transposition puns, metatheses, turnabouts, reversals, marrowskys, and tangle-talk . . . among other things.

Punning, in all its forms, involves the play of words with similar sounds and multiple meanings.

Transposition puns or spoonerisms, to which this book is exclusively devoted, constitute a special type of wordplay, the defining element of which is *linguistic reversal.*

Almost everyone is familiar with the phenomenon. In routine conversation, transpositions are common errors of speech. Such unintentional reversals are a form of *malapropism* (although not every malapropism is a transposition).

When transpositions are uttered by accident, the mind switches words—or *parts* of words—without consciously intending to do so. Often the result is nonsense. But occasionally the process generates new meanings that prove to be intelligible, amusing, or even insightful.

Transpositions may also be *deliberate*. They can be built into jokes that are carefully scripted with a setup and a punch line in which the reversal occurs.

In the pages that follow, examples from both categories abound.

THE APPEAL OF THE PHENOMENON

In a *Time* magazine "Essay" column on slips of the tongue, Roger Rosenblatt dismisses some types of malapropism as uninteresting. But he concedes that "spoonerisms are a different fettle of kitsch."

That's easy for *him* to say! The man is in fine fettle, and obviously has his kitsch in sync. His report, analyzing both the serious and humorous aspects of speech errors, is itself something of a kitschy coup.

According to one theory, humor is created by *incongruity*. This hypothesis certainly applies to transpositions—and to punnery in general—where the contrast between two images is startling or absurd.

The ubiquity of transpositions in popular culture—and their ability to amuse and delight us—is amply demonstrated by their frequent appearance in play, film, and book titles, as well as song lyrics, newspaper and magazine articles, the repartee of comedians and other performers, and many other venues.

The phenomenon occurs not only in English but also in many other (though not all) languages. Among the French, *contrepèterie* is an intellectual and literary sport dating back eight centuries. In German, transpositions are the key components of a verse form called

Schüttelreim. (For some foreign language specimens, see Chapter 9.)

My own fascination with the genre began in childhood. I vividly recall an animated "Popeye" cartoon in which the gruff sailor sighs to Olive Oyl: "Gosh, you're awful pretty." She responds: "Thanks, you're pretty awful yourself."

Even at a tender age, I was intrigued and amused by the fact that the same words, when given a slight spin, could convey such opposite meanings.

I heard Penn State become "state pen," and encountered popular expressions such as "Keep the baby, Faith," "One swell foop," and "That shows to go you." As these examples suggest, I quickly learned to distinguish between reversals that were meaningful, and those that created nonsense.

At some forgotten moment, I began collecting—and devising—transposition puns for fun and profit. I haven't stopped yet.

SOME INTERESTING TERMS AND DEFINITIONS

The word *spoonerism* is an eponym coined from the name of the Reverend Dr. William Archibald Spooner, who is supposed to have committed such gaffes every few minutes. (So goes the legend, but in reality, things were a bit different, as you will learn.)

There is some dispute about the precise meaning of "spoonerism." Some dictionaries and scholars believe the term should be restricted to *accidental* transpositions (thus excluding deliberately crafted jokes). And some authorities maintain that it refers only to the exchange of *initial* sounds (excluding, for example, reversals of whole words within a sentence).

In order to maximize confusion, I will use *spooner-ism* in the broadest sense, interchangeably with *transposition* and *transposition pun*.

Of course, there were spoonerisms prior to Spooner, so it's not surprising that other expressions for the phenomenon exist.

The technical and literary term is *metathesis*. Perhaps this was derived from the graduate student's comment: "I never metathesis I didn't like."

Once upon a time, a spoonerism was called a *marrowsky* (sometimes *marouski* or other variants). The word, reputedly if doubtfully derived from the name of a Polish count who was prone to such blunders, has fallen into disuse of late.

Transpositions are employed by writers and speakers as rhetorical devices—often for emphasis or dramatic effect.

In a *chiasmus* (from the Greek for "crossing"; the first syllable is pronounced like *key*) there are two parallel clauses; the sequence of words in the second reverses that of the first. An example is the phrase "He went off to seek adventure, and off to seek adventure went he." By this definition, any transposition pun that exchanges whole words and states both sides qualifies as chiastic, such as the treacly truism "It's nice to be important, but it's more important to be nice," or the Mae West line "It's not the men in your life, it's the life in your men."

Hypallage (from the Greek for "exchanging"; pronounced "high-*pahl*-uh-jee") is a somewhat archaic term for the reversal of the expected order of words, as in "He took his head away from his hand."

Still another Greek term for literary reversal is *hysteron proteron*, meaning "the latter (put as) the former." Linguistic athlete Willard R. Espy cites this example: "Let us die nobly, and plunge on the foe."

For additional examples of how linguistic reversal can be used to serve serious purposes, see Chapter 10.

Transpositions (the exchange of words or elements thereof) should be distinguished from two other phenomena: *anagrams* (the wholesale rearrangement of letters within a word or sentence) and *palindromes* (words or sentences that read the same both forward and backward).

Why have we explained all this? The answer is plain. It is essential, after all, to know what you are laughing at.

OUR CLASSIFICATION SYSTEM: A TRANSPOSITIONAL TAXONOMY

Linguistic reversal can take several basic *forms*, depending upon the elements that are transposed.

The science of classification can be tricky, but for our purposes things are relatively straightforward. The three most common spooneristic forms involve the exchange of:

> *initial sounds* of words (usually *consonants*), which we shall call *phonemic* transpositions.
> *syllables* or *parts* of words: *syllabic* transpositions.
> *whole* words: *lexical* transpositions.

Here are some illustrations:

For a phonemic transposition, switch the initial sounds of the phrase *peas and carrots* and the result is *keys and parrots*. An appropriate name, perhaps, for a manufacturer of birdcage padlocks.

The syllabic type is less common. An example is the classic punch line *"Putting all your Basques in one exit"* (see page 47).

Lexical transpositions are the quickest to grasp and to recognize. Swap the words in *fat of the land* and you get *land of the fat.* An appealing notion for anyone in the fitness industry.

Lexical transpositions usually result in puns of the familiar homonym variety: same spelling and sound but a different meaning (e.g., *play the float/float the play; spare the change/change the spare*).

Phonemic transpositions are the type that are most commonly *inadvertent,* as in the classic spoonerism. The products of phonemic reversal are *not* homonyms but similar-sounding words that amuse or enlighten due to their balance and rhyme, and the new meanings generated (e.g., *steady as a rock/ready as a stock; wave the sails/save the whales*).

Now consider the phrase *leaving no stone unturned.* This cliché is a spooneristic gold mine, because it can be transposed and redefined in a variety of ways. (Indeed, it *has* been so frequently that crediting originators is impossible.) The first reversal below is phonemic; the second syllabic.

> *No stern untoned.* The determination of the Navy to maintain the appearance of its fleet, or, if you prefer, a crowded nude beach.
> *No tern unstoned.* Mischievous cruelty toward aquatic birds.

The Wall Street Journal gleefully seized upon the second version in a report on ecologists who used a chemical to remove oil from the critters, causing the unexpected side effect of momentary disorientation.

With a slight homophonic shift, we have the merciless drama critic who leaves *no turn unstoned*. Finally, a phonemic variant: Isaac, the famous violinist, leaves *no tone un-Sterned.*

Here are more phrases that can be transposed in multiple ways: "Lot's wife" to "wife's lot" (lexical) or "What's life?" (phonemic). "Rotten to the core" to the unhappy human cannonball's "I don't cotton to the roar" (phonemic) or the disgruntled Marine's "The Corps is rotten to me" (lexical).

All three varieties of transposition—phonemic, syllabic, and lexical—inhabit these pages in profusion. You'll also encounter a few specimens that, like those above, reverse in multiple ways.

PSYCHOLOGICAL AND LINGUISTIC ANGLES

Are transpositions useful only for amusement? Have they no other socially redeeming value?

Lot on your knife! Spoonerisms suggest surprisingly serious stuff. (Try that five times fast.) Consider some of the important questions they raise:

What makes these puns amusing? Why do people unintentionally transpose words and syllables? What is the nature of the mental process at work when we hear the reversal and automatically switch it back to the original? What does the phenomenon reveal about the mechanisms of thought, speech, and communication? What can we learn from it all?

Naturally, Sigmund Freud had an opinion. In *The Psychopathology of Everyday Life,* he offered an explanation of the causes of slips of the tongue. These lapses are not arbitrary, he insisted, but "arise out of [subconscious] elements which are not intended to be uttered. . . ."

Well, what would you *expect* Freud to say?

This is, of course, the famous "Freudian slip." The speaker who makes an error, according to Sigmund, unwittingly reveals something other than his conscious meaning. He has unlocked submerged conflicts or naughty desires that had been repressed deep within the id (or some such place).

Freud claims that just about *every* blunder has a profound psychological cause. "I almost invariably discover a disturbing influence . . . which comes from something *outside* the intended utterance." This influence is a "thought that has remained unconscious" or a "psychical motive force." Indeed, "the most insignificant and obvious errors in speaking have their meaning. . . ." Not surprisingly, the examples he cites are all interpreted to confirm his hypothesis.

In evaluating this explanation, let us bear in mind the principle of logic known as Occam's Razor (not to be confused with Gillette's): *The simpler and more plausible explanation is more likely to be the true one.*

To illustrate the point, consider these lexical and syllabic spoonerisms by well-known entertainers:

On the *Tonight Show,* Johnny Carson introduced the winner of a "call cowing contest." Jay Leno committed a similar gaffe by garbling the announcement of an athlete's demonstration as "jump-roping." Candice Bergen, in mis-takes for her *Murphy Brown* series (preserved in a CBS "Blooper" special), delivers the line: "I'm gonna take out my paper bands and rubber—" (she caught her mistake before saying "clips").

Other people have uttered such unintended phonemic transpositions as "poppy of my caper" for "copy of my paper," and "sweeter hitch" for "heater switch." Children (and some adults) garble syllables within a word, saying, for example, "aminal" or "irrevelant."

To account for such fluffs, there is rarely a need for intensive analysis of the psyche. Laurence Goldstein of Hong Kong University, wielding Occam's Razor in the scholarly journal *Humor,* supplies a more plausible explanation:

"Substitution blunders . . . appear to be due to interference of the preparatory processing of sounds soon *to be* produced. . . . We appear to *think ahead* to the sounds we shall need to make. . . ."

Linguists of Freud's time drew similar conclusions. And 2,500 years ago, Hippocrates noted that some speech errors occur "because before a thought is expressed, other thoughts arise; before words are spoken, other words are formed."

Some linguists regard the phonemic transposition as a variant (or extension) of a *blend:* the combination of two words into one. (Some blends, or "portmanteau words," as Lewis Carroll called them, have entered the language, e.g., "smog," "motel," and "guesstimate.")

In this view, a transposition is first an error of "anticipation" or "contamination," then it's a blend that is *doubled.* Says researcher Archibald A. Hill: "The sounds are manipulable units, and when a blend forces them out of position in one word, they are bodily transported to another."

On the other hand, a potential transposition can be aborted if the speaker realizes her mistake halfway and corrects herself—or simply stops (as Ms. Bergen did in the instance cited above).

Other possible causes are more dramatic. Speech errors, including spoonerisms, can be triggered by anxiety or alcohol, or by neurological disorders, such as aphasia or dyslexia. (For a proposed medical diagnosis of Spooner, see page 34.) In laboratory experiments, transpositions have been induced by external stimuli, such as the presentation of a list of phrases that fool the subject into expecting a reversal.

Even if we don't swallow the Freudian theory, there is more going on here than eats the my—er, meets the eye.

Victoria A. Fromkin, a professor of linguistics at UCLA, is one of several researchers who is convinced that slips of the tongue hold important clues to the development and structure of language and speech.

In a fascinating article in *Scientific American* magazine, she writes: "As in other communication systems . . . noise in any of the stages or connecting channels involved in speech can distort the original message. Most errors of speech would seem to be the result of noise or interference at the stage of linguistic encoding. Such errors can tell us something about a process that is not otherwise observable. . . ."

Such mistakes, then, can serve as a "window into the mind," revealing how language is learned, organized, and stored.

As far back as the eighth century A.D., Arab linguists recorded and studied speech errors. In the late nineteenth century, several European researchers were enthusiastically doing likewise. Rudolf Meringer irritated his colleagues at the University of Vienna with his habit of writing down every error he heard, along with precise details of the circumstances. But his disagreeable behavior paid off. To this day, Meringer's collection of 4,400 methodically cataloged speech errors is treasured by linguists.

Mistakes in speaking, writes Fromkin, are "constrained by the rules of grammar," and are thus in some ways "predictable and nonrandom." In contrast to the Freudian approach, she explains transposition errors in straightforward neurolinguistic terms:

"When we speak, words are structured into larger syntactic phrases that are stored in a kind of *buffer memory* before segments or features of words are disordered. This storage must occur *prior* to the articulatory stage. . . . This process can be demonstrated by the examination of errors in disordered phrases and sentences." (Emphasis added.)

Drawing from a collection of 18,000 speech errors compiled over several decades, Fromkin cites such genuine spoonerisms as "He threw the window through the clock," "Nerve of a vergeous breakdown," and this gem (fertile fodder for Freudians!): "I broke the whistle on my crotch." (If the intended meaning isn't immediately evident, pronounce the "t" in "whistle.")

In their articles and books, Fromkin and other researchers argue persuasively that speech errors provide a rich source of information about human behavior. Among other things, such lapses confirm the reality of linguistic units and grammatical "laws" that are otherwise not easily examined, and provide insights about how language is acquired, structured, and retrieved.

The *Scientific American* article concludes: "By carefully studying speech errors we can get a view of the discrete elements of language and can see the grammatical rules at work. We also can look into the mental dictionary and get some notion of the complexity of the specifications of words and how the dictionary is organized."

And some people think spoonerisms are just gun and fames!

Now for the psychology of humor. *Why* are these puns so amusing?

When the transposition is accidental, the mind inadvertently switches from the "right" (intended) to the "wrong" (uttered) version. When such a spoonerism is repeated, *or* when a transposition pun is deliberately constructed and narrated, the listener (if all goes well) spontaneously executes the appropriate reversal, this time from the "wrong" to the "right" version.

Something within the mind seeks symmetry and balance. In perceiving both sides of the equation, there is a sense of satisfaction—of *completion* or *resolution.* Psychologists call the process "closure."

This phenomenon applies to puns in general, and to much of humor. It's implicit in the expression "getting the point." (Of course, not everyone does—at least, not always!)

Arthur Koestler coined the term "bisociation," which means *thinking on a double track.* According to Koestler, "the pun is the bisociation of a single phonetic form with two meanings—two strings of thought tied together by an acoustic knot."

When there is a "sudden switch of ideas to a different type of logic or to a new rule of the game," one result may be laughter. The humor lies in the perceived incongruity or absurdity caused by contrast between two incompatible frames of reference.

In an article examining theories of humor, G. B. Milner observes that "a very large number of phenomena that trigger off laughter can be shown to be due to *reversal* of one kind or another." (Emphasis added.) To prove his point, not surprisingly, he quotes a bunch of familiar spoonerisms.

There is another essential component of spooneristic humor. Incorrigible punsters defend the craft by pointing out that puns often display elegance via their *economy*. They concisely pack two meanings into a single word or phrase or image.

The pun is "a labour-saving device. It conserves energy, space and time," observes Walter Redfern, a British professor, in a scholarly book he has concisely titled *Puns*. "The pun is also a bargain: two meanings for the price of one word or phrase; a bonus."

We might add that each *transposition* pun exemplifies this virtue twice over, because it contains not just one but *two* plays on words.

Spoonerisms are special, distinct from other kinds of punnery. For any given word or phrase, a pun can assume an almost infinite number of forms. But a series of words can transpose into a spoonerism in only a few specific ways. Like a sonnet or limerick, then, the spoonerism is an art form that is constrained by rules (about which, more anon).

Spoonerisms, in sum, delight and amuse us because of the new and unexpected significance they reveal. It's almost as if a secret meaning is concealed within the original words—a meaning that is magically "unlocked" by the process of reversal.

A BRIEF HISTORY OF SPOONERISMS

I suspect that the first transposition pun occurred immediately following the invention of the first two words.

A cave dweller might accidentally have said "oog-ugh" instead of "ugh-oog." Well, you can imagine the result! No doubt appreciative Stone Age laughter greeted the unintended double meaning, much to the poor fellow's chagrin.

Somewhat more seriously, Lincoln Barnett, in *The Treasure of Our Tongue,* speculates about the ways early humans enlarged their vocabularies:

"A possible mechanism may be found in the process known as metathesis or blending—the transposition of letters or sounds in a word or sentence, resulting in a 'slip of the tongue.' . . . An analogous process might have abetted the growth of language in prehistoric times."

Indeed, some familiar words evolved in precisely this fashion. "Bird," for example, comes from the Old English *brid.*

Let's fast-forward to 1622, when the first English-language transposition pun occurred—or at least the first that was recorded for posterity.

In *The Complete Gentleman* (a sort of "Miss Manners" guidebook for aspiring yuppies of the period), author Henry Peacham recounts this incident:

"A melancholy gentleman, sitting one day at a table where I was, started up upon the sudden and, meaning to say, '*I must go buy a dagger,*' by transposition of the letters, said: 'Sir, *I must go dye a beggar.*' "

Although the anecdote is usually cited to indicate that the diner misspoke himself, Peacham's context is somewhat ambiguous. He may be telling us that the "error" was quite intentional, and that his table companion was an early stand-up (no pun intended) comic.

In the same paragraph, Peacham advises his would-be gentleman reader: "In your discourse be free and affable, giving entertainment . . . with conceits of wit and pleasant invention, as ingenious epigrams, emblems, anagrams, merry tales, witty questions and answers, *mistakings*. . . ." (Emphasis added.) A number of recommended jokes follow, none very risible by today's standards. After all, we've got David Letterman, Andrew Dice Clay, and Tammy Faye Bakker.

Just in case you were wondering, our observant reporter was Henry Peacham the *younger.* Hank's dad—coincidentally also named Henry Peacham—staked his own claim to fame with *The Garden of Eloquence,* a book defining rhetorical devices (among them *hypallage,* noted earlier).

Let's move on.

Two centuries passed. Throughout this period, the entire civilized world was starving, pleading, frantically crying for transposition puns!

Then came a landmark event: The birth, on July 22, 1844, of the Reverend Dr. William Archibald Spooner, the eponymous Oxonian destined to become the form's most distinguished exponent.

Spooner did utter a documented spoonerism or two. But the legend soon overtook reality, and many of his alleged blunders, though amusing, are (alas!) fictitious.

As mentioned earlier, there were spoonerisms before Spooner. Puns of all sorts were popular in nineteenth-century England, and transpositions in particular were a lively game among London medical students.

The fad may have been sparked by a series of novels, beginning in 1854, about the adventures of an undergraduate at Oxford. (Coincidentally enough, that institution would become Spooner's stomping ground for six decades, but at the time he was only ten years old.) In these tales by "Cuthbert Bede"—a pseudonym for Edward Bradley—a character foreshadows Spooner by uttering unintentional and amusing reversals, such as "poke a smipe" for "smoke a pipe."

Since it was a bit premature to call them spoonerisms, the students' punnery was variously known as "Medical Greek," "Hospital Greek," "Gower-Street Dialect," and "marrowskying."

Across the Atlantic, in America's Old West, transpositions were also a common form of humor. Even Abraham Lincoln indulged in the pastime—presumably when he wasn't busy chopping wood or signing proclamations. (For a sample of Honest Abe's efforts, see pages 114–115.)

Over the past century or so, the English language has geometrically expanded. In 1864, for example, there were around 114,000 words. Today, one dictionary lists 616,500. And that's not even counting all the technical terms and multiple meanings.

Because there are more words, and more *meanings* of words, the potential for transposition punnery (both accidental and intentional) has increased dramatically. The proliferation of the mass media—newspapers, magazines, radio, and TV—has also helped expand the possibilities.

Today, unlimited opportunities for spooneristic fun exist—as I hope the following pages will attest.

THE OFFICIAL RULES

Let's get this straight. There must be round gruels—er, ground rules—for constructing transpositional humor.

"What, rules for jokes?!" Some may grumble that such restrictions are irrelevant, unnecessary, gratuitous, and redundant.

One can almost hear the anguished protests: "That just foils the spun!" "It de-perps the fetus!" "You're simply cutting off your nose to fight your space!"

We respectfully disagree. After all, it's beyond dispute that some jokes work better than others. Some are amusing and satisfying; others are not.

Why? What makes the difference? What constitutes a good transposition pun or joke or story?

Whether a spoonerized punch line "snaps back" spontaneously and agreeably is a function of several factors: the prefatory context or setup, the familiarity of the to-be-inverted phrase (quotation, proverb, title, etc.), the nature and sounds of the words themselves, and the similarity of the transposition (in sound and spirit) to the original.

Shocking as it may seem, some of the most famous and repeated transposition-pun tales shamelessly violate the fundamental canons of humor. (See page 44 for a brief discussion of these offenders.)

Clearly, then, a few guidelines are required to govern the correct structure of the form. The setup and punch line must obey certain principles. These determine which transposition puns are legitimate and which are illegal.

Here then are *Hauptman's Five Laws of Transposition Punnery*:

Rule #1: The basic situation or setup should be uncontrived.

The context of the best jokes is natural and logical. The circumstances must be reasonable and plausible.

It is all too easy to burden a spooneristic tale with a premise that is unbelievable or overly complex. For example, one could postulate that, at a Nevada FDA laboratory, a cough suppressant is tested for safety on the respiratory systems of fish—leading up to the line: "Thar's Hold in them thar gills!" Tempting, but too contrived. Ruled out of order.

How about a film about a mind-clouding British cult, entitled *Haze of Devon*? A steamy hillbilly romance novel called *Cot Under the Holler*? Or a song for people who enjoy inclement weather: "Gang, Gang, the Hail's All Here!"

Of course, you *could* do these things. We can't stop you. But as Richard Nixon said, it would be wrong. So such anemic efforts are summarily banned from these pages.

These contrivances bring to mind the hunter's claim that his dog could retrieve objects from ten miles away. The skeptical response: "That seems rather far-fetched!"

Corollaries: Humor should be *comprehensible* to the widest possible audience. So it's wise to avoid esoteric references. Also, keep things *simple*. Supply sufficient data to establish the situation and the facts to justify the punch line. A bit of "color" for atmosphere is permissible. But rigorously shun all extraneous detail and red herrings.

Rule #2: Use only real words, never invented ones.
Neologisms can be fun, but that's another art form.
Only genuine words are permissible in this game. Fab-
rications are prohibited.

For example, one could envision an adorable Dr.
Seuss–like creature, then relate the tale of an evil
mathematician whose malicious goal is "scaring the
Squirkle." Sorry: illegitimate and illegal.

When proper names are included, it is mandatory
to use only real, well-known living or historical figures, or literary characters.

Thus, *Mr. Dreamlings Builds His Bland House* is un-
acceptable. Not to mention the traditional Christmas
song about "Carol, the ancient yuletide troll" and the
Biblical "coat of Kenny Mullers."

(Of course, if you happen to know a Kenny Mullers,
we'll let you get away with it this one time. But watch
your step!)

Use common, familiar words. Banned are obscure
or esoteric words, technical terms, and the like, because the average listener or reader would stand little
chance of understanding them.

**Rule #3: The spoonerized punch line must *work
both ways*.**
Inspired by the economists' "Law of Pure and Perfect
Competition," I call this rule "The Law of Pure and
Perfect Transposition."

The reversal in the punch line should be intelligible, as should the original, pre-spoonerized reference. The two sides must be meaningful and in balance.

For instance: "Am I my Carruthers' beeper?" just
doesn't make it. It's too strained. And it would be diffi-

cult to construct a context in which to set it up without shameless contrivance.

Some puns are meaningful, but prove infelicitous for grammatical or stylistic reasons.

The Can Who Would Be Ming (Kipling saga of an archeological forgery) falls flat. Equally tepid is *Ringin' in the Seine* (musical version of *The Hunchback of Notre Dame*), which requires an unforgivable mutilation of the French pronunciation. (For another, more elegant title for such a production, see page 70.) We also reject the slogan of the ill-fated Disney aerobics pavilion: "Thou shalt not bear Walt's fitness."

In short, like a marriage or relationship, transpositional humor has to work both ways.

Sadly enough, lurking out there are numerous unbalanced, incomplete, meaningless, and stylistically egregious transpositions. In this volume, we shall eschew them.

Rule #4: Present only *one* side of the equation.
State just the *first* component of the transposition. Allow the listener or reader to "flip" the pun to its counterpart.

The reason? It's more satisfying when there is a "missing piece of the puzzle," deliberately left to be completed by the receiver. This is the "closure" phenomenon we noted earlier.

A bit farther on in this Introduction, we will examine a species of spooneristic humor that violates this rule almost by its nature.

Rule #5: Never repeat a word in the punch line that's already in the setup.

To phrase it another way: "We shall tell no line before its time."

Stand-up comedians know that *surprise* is a key element of humor. When telling a joke, they are careful not to predict, anticipate, or prematurely "telegraph" the ending. Instead, they create an alternative explanation, or use a synonym, in the setup.

Yet this rule is easily—and frequently—ignored by unlicensed, nonprofessional spoonerizers.

For example, one punster tells a joke that concludes with the spoonerized punch line: "The house does not make doctor calls." He begins: "The wife of a Las Vegas doctor telephoned a local casino and asked to have her husband paged. . . ."

He blew it! Yet the mistake was easily avoidable. The simple substitution of the word "physician" in the setup would have improved the joke and made it more elegant.

Of course, we hasten to point out that all laws have *exceptions.* (Even Britannia waives the rules.) This brings us to the final—and perhaps the most important—principle of transposition punnery:

Rule #6: If it works, ignore all of the above rules!

The Army's principle "If it moves, shoot it" might be restated: "If it's funny, laugh at it." The G. Gordon Liddy Corollary: "Anything is justified for the sake of the punch line."

We are not sticklers. Unlike Victor Hugo's Inspector Javert, we do not rigidly insist upon blind obedience to "The Law," irrespective of context or mitigating circumstances. If the net result is amusing, feel free to violate any or all rules—even mine. As Chairman Mao might have said about traditional Chinese garden waterfalls: "Let a hundred bowers flume."

Doesn't this view ream seasonable? Consider:

The first rule forbids contrivances and encourages maximum plausibility. But we can tolerate a margin for the "suspension of disbelief" granted to all storytellers.

Although the rules mandate the use of real words, and prohibit invented ones, spoonerisms are often entertaining even when they are nonsensical. (See, for example, the ingenious monologue by "The Capitol Steps," which begins on page 112.)

The rule on balance can on occasion be violated with impunity. A few specimens in this book do not balance perfectly or transpose with impeccable grammar. But they are so risible that it would be a shame to exclude them.

The commandment forbidding the presentation of both sides of the transposition can at times be broken. In some cases, a listener or reader might not instantly recall the original reference. Thus, a few stories and one-liners in the present collection supply both sides.

And the rule banning the repetition of a word may sometimes be difficult or impossible to obey, because there is no appropriate synonym—or because an alternative description would prove too cumbersome.

In the apt phrase of Walter Winchell, "Let he who is without sin stone the first cast." We must judge every pun in context and respect its rights as an individual.

All that having been said, however, it must be noted that there *is* an Ascending Hierarchy of Transpositional Amusement.

The structure of this hierarchy is as follows, from worst to best: Reversals that create nonsensical words; those generating real words that form a meaningless sentence; those producing real words where the resulting statement makes some sense; and finally (the pinnacle of the art) those that create a new meaning that is insightful or profound.

As for disputes about the legitimacy of any transposition pun, I have unilaterally appointed myself the Supreme Arbiter (or "Regent of the Canon," to borrow a phrase from poet-humorists Anthony Hecht and John Hollander). When in doubt, contact me, in care of my publisher, for a definitive, final, and unappealable ruling.

THEMES AND VARIATIONS

Linguistically and grammatically, what is happening when a transposition occurs?

As with all punnery, sounds remain the same or similar, while spellings or meanings—or both—are alchemically transformed (e.g., *shake of the whip/wake of the ship*). Parts of speech are thrown into a linguistic Twilight Zone. Nouns become verbs; verbs turn into nouns. (*"All You Love Is Need"*—Nietzschean protest song.)

But out of this topsy-turvy process can emerge surprising and amusing results, and even nuggets of wisdom.

In phonemic transpositions, if one of the two words begins with a vowel, the *single existing consonant* is the sole component that shifts. (Although some metaphysicians might argue that the nonexistent vowel sound itself moves.) An example: *power out/our pout.*

Occasionally, *internal* consonants or vowels (rather

than *initial* sounds or syllables) are the elements that reverse. One recorded speech error was *blake fruid* for *brake fluid*. For *your fate is sealed,* someone mistakenly said *your feet is sailed.*

An interesting phenomenon is the transposition *within* a word, where the syllables or phonemes reverse to create a whole new meaning. *Refrain,* for example, becomes *free rein. Whirlybirds* turns into *burly words.* Genuine (but nonsensical) errors of this type include *ephelant, mazagine, canpakes,* and *budbeg.*

Newly created liaisons, elisions, and redivisions are entirely permissible. For example, the name *Damon Runyon* becomes *Raymond Onion. Dan Quayle* transposes to *canned whale* (a shock to environmentalists if not to Japanese gourmets). *Two* liaisons occur in the classic transposition *sauces for his table,* which becomes *stable for his 'orses.* In the Tibetan housewife's chronic lament "Oh, my baking yak!" a "y" sound is revealed that is merely a subtle liaison in the original phrase.

KIDS' STUFF?

Absurdity, riddles, and nonsense verses are traditional elements of children's humor. Transpositions, too. And why not?

Tongue twisters such as "She sells sea shells by the seashore" (already spoonerized) generate laughter as a consequence of the inevitable garbling and reversal of the sounds when these sentences are uttered.

In his book *Get Thee to a Punnery,* my friend and fellow Intrepid Linguist Richard Lederer observes: "Many English speaking children first learn how to spoonerize by hearing and posing a special kind of riddle that begins with the formula *"What's the difference between . . . ?"*

These riddles used to be called *conundrums* (not to be confused with condominiums or condoms). Here are three examples, from a book called *1800 Riddles, Enigmas and Conundrums,* by Darwin A. Hindeman:

> What's the difference between a fisherman and a lazy student? One baits hooks; the other hates books.
> . . . an instructor and a locomotive engineer? One trains the mind; the other minds the train.
> . . . a cat and a comma? One has claws at the end of its paws; the other its pause at the end of its clause.

The problem with jokes like these is that they flagrantly violate several rules of transpositional humor. First, they are contrived almost by their nature. Indeed, they are usually cast in this form precisely because it is difficult or impossible to devise a logical context or setup. Another infraction: they usually supply *both* sides of the pun.

It might be said that these riddles constitute a primitive form of humor—sort of the way alchemy represents an early stage of chemistry. But if puns of this type spark an interest in transpositions among children, well and good. There may yet be hope for mankind.

I like to have my Kate and Edith, too (as a bigamist once said), so a few jokes of this genre are included in the present collection—*if* they possess some other redeeming value. (*Caveat:* Some "difference between" jokes are sexually oriented; these specimens are probably *not* suitable for children; see Chapter 7.)

THE MORAL AND INTELLECTUAL STATUS OF PUNNERY

Are puns a low or a high form of humor? The debate rages on.

The entertainment and recreational aspects aside, "puns keep us on the alert," contends Professor Redfern in his book *Puns*. "All humour, and much intelligence, entails an ability to think on two planes at once."

Notes lexicographer Robert Schleifer, in a spooneristic mood: "It takes brains and creativity to patch a Hun."

At still another level, it seems beyond dispute that the appeal of wordplay is directly correlated with intelligence and education. A knowledge of and appreciation for language, and the requisite vocabulary, are all essential for "getting the point." Indeed, puns are incomprehensible unless the listener or reader fully understands *both* meanings. This is especially true for sophisticated puns with literary references.

As corroborating evidence, consider the fact that many members of Mensa, the high-IQ society, are shameless punsters. What's more, they seem particularly fond of transpositions and spoonerisms. Their newsletters and magazines often include "shaggy-dog" stories, and a number of collections of these jokes have been published under their auspices.

"Puns may be a low form of humor," notes the preface to one such volume, "but Mensa people are word people and delight in them."

Another view I find appealing is that of John S. Crosbie, founder of the International Save the Pun Foundation (yes, there is one). Show people how to have fun with words, Crosbie says, and they may be motivated to read. It's one approach to solving the problem of functional illiteracy.

ATTRIBUTION, ORIGINALITY, AND SIMULTANEOUS CREATION

I approach this next task with fixed mealings—er, mixed feelings.

Let's face it. Some people are a credit to their race, while others are in a race to their credit.

I have made valiant efforts to track down original sources. Where documented proof of originality exists (such as a published citation with no known antecedents), I have granted credit accordingly. Occasionally, in cases of creative variation, I have allowed multiple credits.

But one pun anthology suggests the daunting obstacles I faced: "Of course, this type of joke did not begin with [us]. Some of them have been around for centuries. Some are so obvious that they have originated independently time and again."

Tell me about it! Independent creation and inadvertent duplication are pervasive phenomena. After all, most words are in the public domain. Any linguistic adventurer may stalk the elusive phrase, seize upon the quarry, and execute the appropriate reversal and redefinition.

If Newton and Leibniz could independently and simultaneously discover calculus, two punsters can observe that "ports of call" is transposable into "courts of Paul," or "sour pickles" into "power sickles," or "New Kids on the Block" into "new bids on the clock."

Take it from me (or make it from tea): Confirming originality and crediting properly are thankless tasks.

Equally maddening are the many occasions I have devised a clever pun (transposition or otherwise), only to see it appear in print months or years later, attributed to another equally witty and brilliant person. On such occasions I invariably exclaim, "Pete to the bunch!" (or words to that effect).

If you note any mistakes in attribution, remember that it was infeasible to locate *every* published citation, much less every evanescent conversation. To those uncredited or otherwise slighted, I offer apologies.

Everyone deserves a share fake! If there are oversights, let me know. Like the new owner of orthopedic shoes, I shall stand corrected. I will endeavor to rectify such lapses in a future edition or sequel.

(*Will* there be a sequel? Heats the bell out of me! But I'll peep you coasted.)

SOME CAVEATS BEFORE
THE JOKES BEGIN

Attention: The Introduction ends at the next freeway exit. We're about to encounter serious humor. From now on, there's no burning tack.

In this book are more transposition puns and spoonerisms than you can stake a Schick at—as we used to say in the electric razor industry.

You will find clever one-liners, amusing definitions, risible quotes, witty citations in the news and the arts, "shaggy-dog" stories with mangled morals, extended "multiple-pun" pieces, X-rated puns, limericks and other verse, foreign-language reversals, and turnabouts that are illuminating and insightful.

A word of caution: Like truffles, caviar, and other rich delicacies, transposition puns are best consumed in moderation. They should be savored in small portions, not gorged in massive amounts. Overindulgence may be dangerous.

So peruse this book at leisure. Pick it up from time

to time and browse. Savor each specimen as an oenophile would a fine Chardonnay.

Of course, not every entry will necessarily be to your liking. If you encounter a specimen that makes you groan instead of chuckle, just remember the words of Harry Winston: "They can't all be gems!"

A final warning: According to some researchers, spoonerisms are contagious! So be careful.

That is how things stand—in whack and blight, the whole wall of backs, for wetter or burse.

Can *you* come up with a superior example of transpositional humor—either original or one you've heard or read? As you leaf through these pages, you may exclaim, as did the marathon swimmer, "There must be a wetter bay!"

If so, as a Dutch plumber might advise, "Go thou and loo dikewise." Stake your claim—or if you are carnivorous, claim your steak. You have free rein, so don't refrain.

Submit your candidates to me, c/o Dell Publishing, 666 Fifth Avenue, New York, N.Y. 10103.

Meanwhile, you are in for some mental exercise. The chapters that follow constitute a punning wrath along which your intellect may jog. Teasing out the reversals and untying the twists will keep your brain as tarp as a shack.

As Bill Bailey might have put it, the volume you hold is "nothin' but a fine couth tome." Like an S&M party, it's bound to be fun—and fun to be bound. Read and enjoy!

DON HAUPTMAN
New York, N.Y.

CHAPTER
1
Tips of the Slung

Spooner's Spoonerisms, Broadcast Bloopers, and Inadvertent Utterances

Thud & blunder! Here is a collection of unintentional (or allegedly so) transpositions—those tongue-twisting lapses of speech which all of us commit from time to time.

Of course, it would be unforgivable not to commence with the Reverend Dr. William Archibald Spooner, who lived from 1844 to 1930. (Or was it 1930 to 1844?)

Characteristically, Spooner never got around to completing his memoirs. But a fine biography by Sir William Hayter, aptly entitled *Spooner*, was published in 1977.

"All his life, Spooner looked like a white-haired baby," Hayter tells us. "He was small, pink-faced and an albino, with a disproportionately large head and very shortsighted pale blue eyes."

For sixty-two years (1862–1924), Spooner was associated with New College, Oxford—first as an undergraduate, then as fellow, tutor, dean, and warden (a title equivalent to the president of an American school). He was also an Anglican priest; hence the honorific "Doctor," for Doctor of Divinity.

Although he published little of enduring significance, Spooner was a respected (and sometimes feared) personage at Oxford. He was a driving force behind the reform and renaissance of New College, transforming it from what Hayter calls "a narrow and degraded institution" in the 1850s into a successful and prestigious school.

Spooner's students and colleagues, some of whom later achieved considerable distinction, remembered him with affection. Their memoirs portray him as wise and competent. He could be stern but also exceptionally kind. He fit, in many ways, the familiar "Mr. Chips" stereotype of the British headmaster.

Julian Huxley (the biologist, and brother of Aldous) was a New College fellow for six years. In a 1942 article (later reprinted in his book *On Living in a Revolution*), he recalled Spooner as "a good scholar and a good teacher" who possessed "that rare quality which I can only describe as saintliness." Huxley conceded Spooner's eccentricities, but concluded in a 1970 memoir: "In spite of these various handicaps, he became a worthy and respected Warden, and successfully administered the College's affairs for many years."

Historian Arnold Toynbee, in *Acquaintances,* characterized Spooner in these colorful words: "He looked like a rabbit [some say he was the model for Lewis Carroll's White Rabbit], but he was as brave as a lion. He was prepared at any moment to stand up to anybody, however formidable."

"It is certainly ironical," comments Hayter, "that the man who received, and merited, [such] tributes from eminent men . . . should now be chiefly remembered for . . . trivial absurdities, most of them apocryphal. . . ."

Yes, the Spooner story has for too long been clouded by myth and legend. What is the truth? Let us strip away the decades of rumor and innuendo, and—once and for all—get to the mart of the hatter!

In an editorial on the Vice President, *The New York Times* observed: "Dan Quayle has made so many quotable bloopers . . . that he gets tagged even for things he didn't say."

And so it was with the much-maligned Reverend Dr. Spooner. He did commit a few transpositional gaffes. But the legend soon outstripped reality, and most of the slips for which he is credited (or blamed), though amusing, are (unfortunately!) fictitious.

"I was always hoping to hear him utter a spooner-ism, but never did," reminisced a New College student decades afterward.

Ironically, Spooner's *genuine* slips and confusions were mostly of other sorts. He was guilty of malaprop-isms, absent-minded blunders, and inverted logic of the Gracie Allen variety. He had trouble remembering names, and miswrote as well as misspoke.

For example, he once called a famous Irish play *"The Ploughboy of the Western World."* At a dinner, he attempted to clean up spilled salt by pouring wine over it (the opposite procedure was a familiar house-hold hint). After meeting a grieving widow, he whis-pered to a friend: "Very sad; her late husband—eaten by missionaries." And then there was the occasion he invited a colleague to a social gathering to meet Stan-ley Casson, the new fellow. "But *I* am Casson!" was the astonished reply. Spooner's rejoinder: "Never mind; come all the same."

Some Spoonerian scholars theorize that because

nervousness and poor eyesight are among the symptoms of albinism, such afflictions contributed to the warden's slips and other idiocyncrasies. In 1976, a Dr. Potter studied Spooner's life and manuscripts, and hypothesized that he may have suffered from a "developmental disorder" related to dyslexia.

One wag has amplified the legend by suggesting that Spooner started out as a bird-watcher and ended up a word-botcher. In any event, his predicament must have been especially awkward since, as a churchman, he was undoubtedly required to mind his keys and pews.

Oxford lore holds that Spooner admitted to only one spoonerism. Announcing the hymn "Conquering Kings Their Titles Take," he supposedly misspoke and said "Kinkering Congs."

Hayter's biography casts doubt upon this incident, but other witnesses swore they heard Spooner say "The weight of rages will press hard upon the employer," "in a dark, glassly," and "chase the train of thought." According to another reasonably authenticated account, he introduced Dr. Child's friend as "Dr. Friend's child."

If these lapses really occurred, they were certainly pardonable. But college students in those days were as mischievous as they are today. The reverend doctor's occasional clerical errors (no pun intended) sparked a fad that would make subsequent campus sports like goldfish swallowing appear insignificant by comparison.

In the beginning, there was Dr. Spooner's Word. And lo, it came to pass that wits and comedians began inventing transposition puns and passing them off as genuine Spooner bloopers.

"We used to spend hours in inventing 'spooner-isms,'" recalled a New College alumnus in 1930.

The craze spread like filed wire—er, wildfire. By 1885, Oxonians had coined the term "spoonerism." Before the century turned, the word was in everyday use throughout England.

In due course, the clergyman was "quoted" as having perpetrated such blunders as these:

"Blushing crow" for "crushing blow."

"A well-boiled icicle" for "well-oiled bicycle."

"The cat popped on her drawers" for "the cat dropped on her paws."

"I have in my bosom a half-warmed fish" (for "half-formed wish"). This supposedly occurred in a speech welcoming Queen Victoria.

"Our dear old queen" then underwent a sex change and became "Our queer old dean."

After dropping his chapeau: "Will nobody pat my hiccup?"

He advised a friend on a shopping expedition to "steal at the doors."

At a wedding: "It is kisstomary to cuss the bride."

Preparing for an ocean voyage, he searched for "some crooks to take on a booze."

At the end of World War I: "When the boys come home from France, we'll have the hags flung out."

Visiting a friend at his country cottage: "You have a nosy little cook here."

To a guest arriving in inclement weather: "Hush that brat; it's roaring pain outside!"

Paying a visit to a school official: "Is the bean dizzy?"

Addressing a group of farmers: "Ye noble tons of soil."

This classic is often cited: "Mardon me padom, you are occupewing my pie. May I sew you to another sheet?"

In his sermons, the Gospels' "cheerful tidings" supposedly became "tearful chidings." "From Greenland's icy mountains" was transformed into "From Iceland's greasy mountains." The prodigal son was "on the busy drink of destruction." And of course, he assured his flock that "the Lord is a shoving leopard."

After all that, no wonder he reportedly sighed: "It is beery work preaching to empty wenches!"

Some skeptics grumble that the accidental transpositions attributed to Spooner *must* be spurious because, after all, they sound "too perfect."

"There is something distinctly odd" about them, says one linguist. "They always make sense." And here is Toynbee's Theorem: "The wittier or more elegant the specimen, the less likely it is to be authentic."

These objections sound plausible, but they overlook what I call the Darwinian/Spencerian Evolutionary Postulate of Spoonerisms: He might have uttered lots of others, but only the fittest survived.

Some suspicions are justified, however. Perhaps the most dubious story of all (one only wishes it had really occurred!) concerns the stern reprimand Spooner allegedly delivered to a misbehaving student:

"You have hissed all my mystery lectures. You have tasted two worms. I saw you fight a liar. Pack up your rags and bugs, and leave immediately by the town drain!"

What was Spooner's reaction to all this? Like Queen Victoria, he was not amused by these tales scold out of tool—er, told out of school.

One evening, a group of carousing students celebrating an athletic victory gathered beneath his window and loudly called for the Reverend to address them. (By some accounts, this happened at an alumni dinner. Take your choice.)

"You don't want a speech," he answered testily. "You only want me to say *one of those things.*" (Regrettably, he didn't say "thun of those wings.")

Back to that *New York Times* editorial about Vice President Quayle, which concludes: "Some stories may seem too good not to be true. But even if funny, they're false."

Oh, well. We still owe Dr. Spooner a debt of gratitude for unwittingly popularizing a form of wordplay that is, to borrow a phrase from W. S. Gilbert, "a source of innocent merriment." Julian Huxley lauded Spooner as "a man who was the direct or indirect cause of a considerable addition to the world's stock of good-natured laughter."

In 1979, the now-departed *Quest* magazine proposed that the Good Doctor's birthday, July 22, be designated "Spooner's Day." He would be honored annually with a 21-sun galute.

The advent of broadcasting created exponentially greater possibilities for accidental transpositions, along with the technology to capture and preserve them for posterity.

The late Kermit Schafer, a producer in the early days of radio and TV, made a hobby of collecting on-air "bloopers." During the 1950s, he turned his avocation into a thriving commercial venture, churning out numerous books and LP records.

Schafer claimed that every gaffe in his archive was "authentic." Maybe so, but it's obvious to any listener with an IQ over room temperature that a lot of the boners he marketed on vinyl were recreated by actors. Despite these doubts, many specimens in his collection are amusing.

Of course, not every blooper is a spoonerism (nor, by our definition, is every spoonerism a blooper). But here are some of Schafer's examples which qualify:

> On a Canadian radio station, a hapless retail store sponsor was identified as a "drug and rape shop."

> Dialogue on a crime drama: "How'd you get caught?" "Some dirty squeal pigeon stooled on me."

> A commercial for a rodent killer promised listeners that it would wipe out "all mats and rice." (Probably wouldn't sell in Tokyo.)

> On the BBC, "the Pump Room at Bath" became "the bathroom at Pump."

That brings to mind the day Dave Garroway told NBC viewers: "You'll find Dial soap a refreshing addition to your schlub or tower."

A horror movie was "guaranteed to make your ends stand on hair."

From a newscast: "The rumor that the President would veto the bill is reported to have come from a high White Horse souse."

Another commercial: "This king-size refrigerator is large enough to seat all the nudes of your family."

The last item is an interesting instance of the transposition of *internal vowels* rather than initial consonants. That distinction is shared by three famous flubs involving famous names: Radio announcer Harry von Zell introduced the President of the United States as "Hoobert Heever." Attributed to a Massachusetts announcer: "The Duck and Doochess of Windsor." And Lowell Thomas identified a British politician as "Sir Stifford Crapps."

Occasionally, a lexical (whole-word) transposition exactly reversed the intended meaning. A pianist, the radio audience was informed, "plays passages of ease with the greatest of difficulty." A money-back guarantee was underscored with the enthusiastic pledge: "You have everything to lose and nothing to gain." And a clothing store commercial urged: "Always shop at Robert Hall, where prices are high and quality is low." (This may help explain why the chain is now defunct.)

There was also the appetizing "Betty Baker's crock mix," a public service reminder to "Be sure to get your pork Solio vaccine," and the corporation that was rechristened "Hell and Bowel."

Schafer confessed to at least one transpositional blooper of his own. One of his books is titled *Your Slip Is Showing!* On an interview program, he claimed, he announced the title as *Your Ship Is Slowing.* (At that point, of course, he might have told the host: "Your show is slipping"—see page 63.)

"The unintended spoonerism is a bane of broadcasters," writes Norman Ward in *Verbatim, The Language Quarterly*. Indeed. But film and tape ultimately came to dominate broadcasting, and this change diminished the likelihood that "live" bloopers would escape over the airwaves.

Hollywood's entrepreneurs, however, were not to be thwarted by that detail. Following in Schafer's footsteps, and in the spirit of environmental recycling, they rummaged through rehearsal tapes, "outtakes," and other cutting-room-floor ephemera, searching eagerly for entertaining mistakes.

Broadcast bloopers thus found new life in videotapes for sale and rental, and in TV specials commanding huge national audiences, presided over by such luminaries as Ed McMahon and Dick Clark. So we can expect a bright future for the art.

Performers on the legitimate stage are no less prone to error. When Rex Harrison died, obituaries recalled his first role. He played a new father and managed to muff his one line. "It's a doctor!" he shouted. "Fetch a baby!"

In an amateur performance during the early 1900s, another actor (whose name charitably has been lost to posterity) had to announce that "The queen has swooned." He said "The swoon has queened," then "The sween has cooned," and finally "The coon has sweened."

William Safire's popular *New York Times Magazine* language column told of the Reagan administration official who evidently confused the expressions "no free lunch" and "no quick fix." As a result, she informed a Senate subcommittee: "There is no quick lunch here." (Unfortunately for our purposes, she neglected to say anything about a free fix.)

To become a real aficionado of the form, it is advisable to get an early start. A *Reader's Digest* anecdote reports that a youngster, having his teeth examined for the first time, inquired if the assistant performing the prophylaxis was the "gentle high dentist" his parents had told him about.

As for myself, I still say "Art is seldom as satisfying as life" when I really mean the opposite (I think).

CHAPTER
2
Stowing Thrones

Fractured Fables,
Mangled Morals, and
Shaggy Dogs

When transposition puns are crafted for purposes of amusement, they are often built into elaborate stories that end with punned punch lines. These yarns are also known as "shaggy-dog" stories.

Of course, not all tales (or tails) of the shaggy-dog species employ *transposition* puns. In this chapter, we'll focus exclusively on those that do.

Science fiction buffs and members of Mensa use the term "Feghoots" to describe the genre. The word was serendipitously coined during a Scrabble game by writer Reginald Bretnor, who for purposes of punnery employs the anagrammatic pseudonym Grendel Briarton.

In Bretnor/Briarton's very short stories, Ferdinand Feghoot is a picaresque character who travels "through time and space," finding adventures that invariably seem to culminate in punned or spoonerized morals. Examples: "Beware of geeks baring grifts" and, in a nod to the popular opus of his colleague Frank Herbert, "What is so rare as a jay in *Dune*?"

Puns and spoonerisms (ranging from ingenious to

awful) may also be found in the works of such prominent science fiction writers as Isaac Asimov (see page 50), Keith Laumer, and Spider Robinson.

Across the Atlantic, similar acts are perpetrated by the popular BBC radio show *My Word!*, which has been on the air since 1957. Panelists Frank Muir and Denis Norden are each handed a well-known quotation, and must ad-lib an outrageous tale that concludes with a punned (occasionally spoonerized) version of the quote. One such punch line (the buildup for which, in leisurely British fashion, runs more than eight hundred words): "His bird is as good as his wand."

Some "mangled moral" transposition tales have been repeated and reprinted so often that they have become "classics" of the genre.

But the achievement of legendary status is no guarantee of quality. Several of the most familiar stories are rather shabby excuses for humor, hopelessly contrived and shamelessly violating the Transposition Laws we outlined in the Introduction.

You may recognize one or more of the following (alleged) jokes, which I shall dispense with as quickly as possible.

Have you heard the ones about . . .

Fictitious baseball players ("the beer that made Mel Famey walk us"); fashionably attired creatures from other planets ("the furry with the syringe on top"); piscatorial pickpockets ("carp-to-carp walleting"); instrument repairmen improbably named Oppornockity (he don't tune twice!); disappointing diving discoveries ("a gritty pearl is like a malady");

and sheiks who ride carousels and then . . . well, never mind ("Middle lamb, you've had a dizzy bey").

Even the ancient and endlessly reiterated tale of the "boyfoot bear with teak of Chan" rings hollow in its attempted double-pun moral because of the inevitable contrivance needed to set up the first of the two components of the punch line.

We have cataloged the above for the historical record. That task accomplished, we summarily expunge these groaners from the canon of transpositional humor!

Happily, though, other "classic" spoonerized tales are far superior. I suspect that it would be impossible to ascertain definitively the identities of their creators. I recall many from my childhood, and they appear in numerous anthologies of humor and punnery. In some cases, I am retelling them with my own liberal revisions to the setups.

The Sioux Indian chief envied the wealthy socialites who, each summer, visited his island reservation in their magnificent yachts. He could never afford these luxuries himself, but he wanted his children to experience such an affluent life. He worked hard to put them all through Ivy League schools. He knew he had achieved his dream when he saw his red sons in the sail set.

Once upun a time, long before due process and the Miranda Warning were discovered, a king became convinced that a member of his court was betraying state secrets to the enemy. He called them all together and demanded that the traitor confess. No one spoke. "I will behead each of you until the rogue admits his guilt!" roared the king.

Still no response. Whop! The first unlucky victim lost his head. Then another. The third suddenly cried: "Wait! I did it!" But it was too late, and he too met his fate by the executioner's blade. *The moral?* Don't hatchet your counts before they chicken.

In the early years of unmanned space exploration, NASA experts determined that monkeys were not genetically suited for certain zero-gravity experiments. To rectify the problem, the scientists requisitioned twelve holstein cows from the Department of Agriculture, loaded them (with some difficulty) aboard a satellite, and launched it into orbit. The animals became known as the herd shot round the world.

During the height of the popularity of *Going My Way* and other movies with religious themes, two Hollywood agents visited a famous convent to acquire the film rights to its story. Removing the contract from his briefcase, the younger of the pair, overly eager, began chatting excitedly about residuals, royalties, and the like. He failed to realize that this was precisely the sort of materialistic talk that was bound to turn off the conservative Mother Superior whose approval was essential to the deal. Finally, his more experienced colleague took him aside and whispered: "Wait 'til the nun signs, Shelly."

The maharajah of an Indian province outlawed the killing of tigers. Soon, the enraged and endangered citizens revolted and deposed him. It was the first recorded instance of reign called on account of game.

If this next yarn sounds familiar, perhaps it's because it's the one that gave Ralph Kramden so much trouble in a perennially rerun *Honeymooners* episode.

Once upun a time, Sir Lancelot was journeying back to Camelot. Suddenly, a drenching storm erupted. In the muddy, rain-soaked path, his horse tumbled and broke a leg. Lance was furious but unhurt. Espying a nearby cottage, he trudged to the door and knocked loudly. "I must return to the Round Table at once!" he shouted. "Give me a horse!" The door was opened hesitantly by a terrified but humble peasant. "Sire," he quavered, "we are merely terrified-but-humble peasants. We possess no such equine luxuries." Sir Lancelot pointed to an unusually large and mangy Great Dane tethered nearby. "Under the circumstances, I have little choice. Saddle up that beast and I shall ride him home." "Your lordship," quoth the peasant, "I wouldn't send a knight out on a dog like this."

The punch line of the following story is often preceded by a complicated setup involving a crowded theater, revolving door, "narrow mountain pass," or the like. But there is a far more elegant context that builds upon a true historical incident.

After the Carlist War in 1876, Spain and France divided the Euzkadi homeland in the Spanish Pyrenees. To avoid conscription by the Spaniards, many residents fled to America. Notes a recent article: "By paying a fee, a man could leave the country and return later without the stigma of desertion." The emigrants hoped to find gold in California, repay their debts, and return to their native land. Alas, as we know, not all newly arrived fortune-seekers struck it rich. The refugees were left stranded. *The moral?* Don't put all your Basques in one exit.

A man dies and ascends to heaven. One day, he sees a distinguished looking elderly fellow with a long white beard walking around, attempting to examine each resident with a stethoscope, each of whom rebuffs the interloper with annoyance. "Who is that?" the newcomer asks St. Peter. "Oh, don't pay any attention to *him,*" Pete replies. "That's just God playing doctor."

Once upun a time, a Nigerian tribal chief was so beloved by his people that they presented him with a magnificent jewel-encrusted ceremonial chair as a symbol of their loyalty and affection. At the unveiling, the chief expressed his gratitude. He then announced that such a treasure was not suitable for everyday use, but only for high occasions of state. Therefore, he had decided to store the gift in a distant thatched hut, whence it would be removed only for holidays and other important events. But that very night, tragedy struck: the hut caught fire. In the conflagration, all of its contents were destroyed. *Moral*: People who live in grass houses shouldn't stow thrones.

Here are some tales of more recent vintage, along with attributions. (Although, as I noted in the Introduction, others may well have gotten there earlier.)

An American soldier stationed in Germany admired a beautiful antique beer mug. He could not resist purchasing it, despite its exorbitant price and obvious fragility. Upon returning home, he carefully placed it in a recess in his living-room wall. In spite of several furious battles with his wife, his treasured memento remained intact. Why was it preserved from harm? Because a niche in time saves stein.

> —William Olmstead,
> quoted in *Saturday Review*

(In a clever short story by Isaac Asimov, a criminal exploits the statute of limitations by escaping to the future, thus, "A niche in time saves [Montie] Stein." In yet another variant, a noted author avoids being struck by a car when she stops to scratch a mosquito bite, hence: "An *itch* in time saves [Gertrude] Stein.")

A farmer was having trouble with Nellie, his old horse. She had an unusually long mane, and birds had begun nesting in it. Nellie was getting skittish as a result, and the farmer complained about it one day at the general store. "Shucks," said a friend, "I can tell you how to stop that. Just sprinkle baker's yeast in her mane every night for a week." So the farmer did, and sure enough the birds quit bothering old Nellie. The following Saturday, the farmer asked his friend why it worked. "Well now, I thought everybody knew that," the old gentleman answered. "Yeast is yeast, and nest is nest, and never the mane shall tweet."

> —William Brodnax, quoted by Lydel Sims in the Memphis *Commercial Appeal,* retold in *Reader's Digest.* (A variant was invented by radio's "Colonel Stoopnagle"; see page 111.)

A gorgeous actress visits a chiropractor and complains of an injured knee. Examining his new patient, the doctor asks: "What's a joint like this doing in a nice girl like you?"

> —A line in *Kiss Me Stupid,* the beleaguered 1964 Billy Wilder comedy. (In a popular variant, the query is uttered by a parent who discovers his daughter smoking marijuana.)

The football coach had two troublesome players who drank on the road—in blatant violation of his strict rules. One evening he suspected that the misbehaving pair might be in the hotel bar. Just as he entered, he glimpsed the two offenders slipping off their chairs to hide in the lavatory. "What'll it be, sir?" asked the bartender. "A ginger ale," replied the coach, "and see what the backs in the boys' room will have."

> —retold by Bennett Cerf and Art. Moger

A neighborhood bakery produced excellent bread in huge quantities for its eager customers, who invariably wanted their purchases sliced. It proved a huge chore for the overworked owner, an old-fashioned type who did everything by hand. For a solution to his problem, the baker searched everywhere. At last, he discovered just the tool he needed. His delighted customers congratulated him on his good luck in finding a four-loaf cleaver.

> —from a Bennett Cerf collection, slightly recast

Two policemen spot a car driven by a man in a convict's outfit. They pull him over and make an arrest. At the station, however, the cops discover that he is a distinguished court official on his way to a costume ball. *Moral*: Never book a judge by his cover.

> —*The Complete Pun Book,* by Art. Moger. (The punch line became the title of a 1990 anthology of "outrageous puns" by Theodore A. Brett.)

A newspaper writer complains that he must repeatedly endure hearing his readers telling him the same anecdotes that appeared in his column. "It's the tale dogging the wag."

> —*Punch,* the English humor magazine. (In another version, an unattractive woman has a jealous crush on a handsome comedian and surreptitiously follows him around—or the dog tailing the wag.)

The chef had an annoying habit of turning up the temperature on the steam table, causing his fellow workers considerable discomfort. Asked why he did it, he shrugged and replied: "I'm simply adding more mist to the grill."

—quoted in *Saturday Review*

190,000,000 years ago, at the beginning of the Jurassic period, cave children loved to hop onto the back of a friendly Stegosaurus, whose distinctive high-arched body reached twenty feet. One day, to his parents' horror, a toddler leaped off a precipice, oblivious to the fact that, seconds before, the great beast below had lumbered off. "Poor kid," said his father, shaking his head, "he hasn't got a Steg to land on."

—Lewis Burke Frumkes

A group of sailors, on leave in New Orleans for the first time, enthusiastically set off for the bars on Bourbon Street. But one fellow demurred; he was determined to visit the fashionable Garden District restaurant he had heard so much about. His suggestion prompted derisive laughter from his shipmates. "You ought to know," they taunted, "keel men don't eat *riche.*"

—Lewis Burke Frumkes

A rock group on tour is motoring through Wyoming in its luxurious recreational vehicle. Suddenly, their passage is obstructed by hundreds of steers. The musicians hail a cowboy and politely ask if they may drive through in order to meet their concert date. "No way," snaps the cattleman. The rockers huddle to consider their options, then return to the stubborn cowboy. "We've got some really unusual grass," they offer slyly. "Marijuana in suppository form." The cowhand accepts the bribe and reins in his animals long enough to allow the group's bus to proceed. *Moral?* A herd in the band is worth boo in the tush.

—*National Lampoon*

The following group is from The *New York* Magazine Competition. (The first four were prizewinners.)

An impressionable New England college girl dropped out of school to live with a handsome young man whose main attraction was his smoldering dark gaze. Within six months, however, she was abandoned and heartbroken. She loved not Wellesley but two eyes.

—Helen K. Weil, Larchmont, N.Y.

(Bennett Cerf related a variant in which the coed sacrifices her studies to make frequent visits to a pair of YMCAs. Ms. Weil's subsequent version is far more ingenious.)

John James Audubon, pursuing an intense interest in the genetic traits of birds, raised a colony of European crows. One day, he met a friend who inquired: "Bred any good rooks lately?"

—Michael Deskey, New York, N.Y.

(The above pun inspired the title of a 1986 shaggy-dog anthology by James Charlton, to which the horrifically successful author Stephen King independently contributed a similar tale.)

We were creeping through hostile jungle, well camouflaged. I was covered with vines. My wife wore twigs. And so we pressed on bravely with sod on our guide.

—Anthony Gray, Closter, N.J.

A wealthy German businessman presented his new bride with a beautiful fur coat. But he was unaware that she opposed the use of animals for such purposes. Seeing her dismay, he immediately bought a cloth garment in order to soothe his beavered frau.

—Barbara Allen, Kings Point, N.Y.

At a medical outpost, a native was brought in with a cleanly fractured leg. The assistant applied a leech. When the doctor arrived, he scolded: "Never give an even break a sucker."

—Jack A. Kasman, Yonkers, N.Y.

George Gershwin, vacationing on Cape Cod with several colleagues, couldn't decide whether to rehearse a composition or spend the afternoon cycling along the beach. "Which shall it be?" he asked his friends. "Do we get down to work, or do we bike up the strand?"

—Joseph Gelband, New York, N.Y.

Jack the Ripper's grandmother had a minor behavioral problem of her own. Armed with a switchblade, she attacked visitors to a London public lavatory. Terrified citizens called her the old woman who shivved in a loo.

—Albert G. Miller, New York, N.Y.

The laboratory rat, despite all urging, stubbornly refused to perform the assigned experiments. After a while, however, he reconsidered and wended his maze.

> —Nanette V. Jay, New York, N.Y.

In Moscow, people felt sorry for the urchin who trudged along, bent under his heavy load of newspapers. But little Ivan held his head with pride, because, after all, he did have a clutch of *Tass*.

> —Mary Ann Miller, Columbus, Ohio

Each day, London policemen escort employees of the underground transport system as they carry the receipts to the bank. This ritual is known to tourists as the guarding of the change.

> —Robert Hendrickson, Ozone Park, N.Y.

Madame Scarlatti is attracted to Boutlaire, her new gamekeeper. Although he professes to love her, he appears to love his game more. For when she asks him to capture and bring her an animal as a token, he says: "Frankly, Madame, I don't give a deer."

> —Fred Schreiber, Bronx, N.Y.

The prospector in Nome who sold me his gold claim drew up a map showing how to get there. "Be careful as you pass the grizzly den," he warned. "Isn't there a safer route?" I inquired. "No," he replied. "That's a bear you'll just have to cross."

> —Larry Fine, Forest Hills, N.Y.

The famous Czech film director, fighting a severe cold, was nevertheless on location in Athens, determined to complete his movie. One scene at an ancient ruin required so many takes that Miloš soon developed laryngitis. To this day, locals who worked on the set remember the director as the hoarse Forman of the Acropolis.

—Chris Doyle, Burke, Va.

Wanda obtained an advance copy of the Women's Air Force entrance examination. She was accepted, but authorities subsequently discovered her dishonesty, and her captain discharged her. "Why?" she protested. "Because," the officer answered, "we're separating the cheat from the WAF."

—Barbara Jacobs, Queens, N.Y.

Have you ever had the experience of parking in a one-hour zone, inserting the coins, then finding yourself—fifty-five minutes later—still in line at the bank? At such times, you might suddenly find religion, and fervently pray that you will make your meter!

—Viktor Blume, Sayville, N.Y.
(The pun was anticipated in a lyric by Lorenz Hart.)

Mr. and Mrs. Baruch wanted their son to become a shipping clerk in the family business. But he had loftier ambitions. Worn out by their offspring's determination, they finally gave up. "Oh well," the father sighed. "I guess the Bernie's not for lading."

—Townsend Brewster, Jamaica, N.Y.

The Father of Our Country, in his early years, applied to an Ivy League women's college. His coura-

geous effort served as a turning point in the movement for coeducation. The incident will be
dramatized in a new film entitled *Mr. Washington
Goes to Smith.*

—Inspired by an uncredited entry

Dick Whittington was investigating warring fac-
tions of a Chinese secret society. Suddenly, his pet
was taken hostage! When Dick reported the abduc-
tion to the police, the officers were unsympathetic.
"What's the matter," they teased. "Tong got your
cat?"

—Mary Ann Madden, Competition Editor,
in an example

Here are some soon-to-be-classic stories of my own:

Now that he is retired, the senator has time to
indulge his passion for gourmet cooking. He especially loves to prepare a unique homemade fried
snack, which he distributes to his Indiana neighbors. His culinary skills and generosity are so appreciated that he is greeted daily with the exclamation: "Good chips, Mr. Bayh!"

In the spring of 1968, circumstances required
that student antiwar activist Mark Rudd and his
wife leave town in a hurry. But there was one hitch
to their planned journey: they wanted a set of expensive stereo speakers. The couple was dis-
traught. In desperation, they turned for advice to a
trusted confidant: their favorite professor at Colum-
bia. The sage listened patiently as they explained

their dilemma, then leaned back and rendered his verdict: "Gather ye Bose, Rudds, while ye may."

Early in his career, Mr. Stewart endured a punishing touring schedule. In each city, he performed for six straight days. Then, to culminate each visit, he granted a lengthy interview to the local radio station. Reminiscing about those grueling years, his manager lifted his eyes heavenward, prayerfully intoning: ". . . and on the seventh day, Rod guested."

At Nazi cabinet meetings, one of Hitler's closest associates had a habit of rising unpredictably to utter loud, unsolicited opinions. Finally, the Führer reached his limit. "Sit down, Martin!" he bellowed. From that day on, the hapless officer was known as the Bormann of the Chaired.

For months, a clerk at a music publishing company had been pilfering small sums from his employer's account, expecting to be able to return the money before being found out. One day, however, he realized that he would never be able to make good on his thievery. Frantically, he emptied out the balance and grabbed a plane to Brazil. For a while, the crime went undetected. Then executives became suspicious and called the police. The detective examined the books, eyed the clerk's conspicuously empty desk, and exclaimed: "How long has this been owing? Gone?!"

Which reminds me of the fellow who robbed a bank, then booked luxury-class passage on an ocean liner. In hot pursuit were two policemen. The first night at sea, they observed the miscreant hiding his ill-gotten gains under the tarpaulin of a lifeboat. One officer whispered to the other: "That's what I call stowing in guile!"

Some years ago, Senator Morse devised a patriotic plan to conserve valuable cemetery space. Americans would be encouraged to forgo burial in favor of encasement in translucent resin, much as nature preserves fossils. The bill was roundly defeated by Congress, but the unusual proposal is still remembered as the Amber Graves of Wayne.

The Chinese restaurant owner was dismayed. His children, corrupted by slothful American ways, had abandoned the traditional Old World values of diligence and hard work. One day, while assisting him with the preparations for a large banquet, the kids chatted merrily among themselves, oblivious to their duties. The patriarch could no longer restrain his anger. Turning upon his disobedient offspring, he shouted: "Beware the jabber, son! My wok!"

Finally, even though it probably violates most of my own rules, I cannot resist concluding this fractured fable chapter with the following original composition:

On cold winter nights, Zeke, an elderly Vermont farmer, appreciated nothing more than a roaring fireplace. One evening, however, just after Zeke lit the fire, he fell asleep. Several hours later, jolted from his slumbers by the chill, he realized that the blaze had been reduced to embers. Grabbing a poker, Zeke attempted to stir the flames back to life. At that moment, an errant breeze from the chimney blew the ashes into his face. As a result, his asthma was aggravated and he had to be hospitalized. *The moral?* Die down with logs, and you flake up with wheeze.

CHAPTER
3
Runelight and Moses

Transposition Puns
in Song and Story

There's a broken light for every heart on Broadway.

Entertainment, the arts, and popular culture all constitute fertile sources of transposition punnery.

In 1989, a Broadway revival of *The Threepenny Opera* generated uniformly disastrous reviews. The most scathing criticism was directed at the famous rock star making his stage debut. Some industry wags reportedly were asking "O Sting, where is thy death?"

Heywood Broun, in a similarly peevish mood, is said to have confided to Tallulah Bankhead: "Your show is slipping!"

But excessive harshness would be unfair. As Walter Winchell so temperately counseled: "Let he who is without sin stone the first cast."

John Simon, the usually acerbic theater critic, was evidently in a kinder and gentler mood the night he caught the act of a legendary chanteuse. "What is the horn of plenty," gushed his review, "compared to plenty of Horne?"

Speaking of Walter Winchell, where would show business be without its gossip-mongers? Which reminds me: What's the difference (if any) between the

Stealth Bomber and Kitty Kelley? One has never been tested in battle; the other has never been bested in tattle.

If you're too busy to see *Hamlet,* here is a capsule review: "It's Dane as play!"

From time to time, transposition puns appear as titles of plays, films, and books. For example:

Too True to Be Good is a comedy by George Bernard Shaw.

Blume in Love is a 1973 film written and directed by Paul Mazursky.

Every Little Crook and Nanny is a mystery novel by Evan Hunter (and a movie).

The Clothes Have No Emperor is a satirical volume described as "A Chronicle of the American 80s."

You'll See It When You Believe It is an inspirational self-help book by Wayne Dyer.

Transpositions also pop up in musical theater lyrics, such as the E. Y. Harburg ditty that warns the listener not to "let a kiss fool you" or "let a fool kiss you."

In Cole Porter's "Always True to You in My Fashion" (from *Kiss Me Kate*), an attractive young lady notes the advantages of having a wealthy but older suitor: "If a Harris pat means a Paris hat, okay!" And Porter's "Tale of the Oyster," the amusing biography of a suicidal mollusk, concludes: "Now I've had a taste of society, and society has had a taste of me."

In *Kismet* (libretto by Charles Lederer and Luther

Davis), a wealthy man informs Hajj, the poet-hero (temporarily a panhandler), that he prefers to give alms to a more familiar mendicant. Hajj improvises this reply: "You say you're too old to change beggars?/Your attitude strikes me as strange./It's easy enough to change beggars—/What's difficult is, to beg change."

A lyric by Christopher Gore in *Nefertiti* (which never made it to Broadway) has a tongue-tied princess saying "a stare of fate" for "affair of state." (In the original hieroglyphics, it works even better.)

And the Ira Gershwin/Kurt Weill musical *Firebrand of Florence* contains a song constructed around transposition puns. (The lyrics are reprinted in their entirety beginning on page 122.)

But why should transpositions be restricted only to *existing* works? With a little imagination, we can inject new life into show business. Let's browse through a hypothetical future guide to cultural events:

Entertainment Listings

Tonight's Network Television Fare:

8 PM   2   **Super Barrio Mothers**—In New York's Spanish Harlem, two spunky women (Chita Rivera, Rita Moreno) team up to fight crime and drugs.

4 **"Honey, I Kid the Shrink!"**—
A Hollywood psychiatrist (Bob
Newhart) discovers that his practice
consists entirely of stand-up comics.

7 **Dick and QWERTY**—A former President (David Frye) tries to write his memoirs, but faces constant distractions. In the premiere episode, a balky word-processing program causes trouble.

8:30   2 **"Is My Race Fed!"**—Cherokee grocer (Burt Reynolds) vows to build a supermarket empire.

4 **Lifestyles of Fitch and Ramos**—Sparks fly when a gruff veteran Irish cop (George Kennedy) is reluctantly teamed with a hotheaded young Hispanic partner (Prince).

7 **Lipping the Trite Fantastic**—A presidential speechwriter (Howard Cosell) gets into hilarious scrapes with the press and the White House staff.

9:00   2 **Come Shane or Come Rhine**—Unusual new series dramatizes the adventures of a cowboy and his sidekick, a college professor endowed with extrasensory powers.

4 **Wise and Crispers**—For this telecast, the acclaimed Bergman film has been retitled due to sponsorship by a snack food company.

7 **Pin Tweaks**—A small-town acupuncture clinic and its gallery of odd patients.

13 **The Glue and the Bray**—Shocking documentary on the plight of wild donkeys condemned to death.

Tomorrow Afternoon's Highlights:

12 NOON 13 **A Whale's Christmas at Childs**—This allegorical animated story is destined to become a perennial. In December of 1930, Sam, a lonely sperm whale insurance salesman, finds happiness at a popular Manhattan restaurant. (Voice of Sam: Raymond Burr.)

4:30 7 **A Love Only a Mother Could Face**—(After-school Special) Gay teenager comes out of the closet and finds his parents surprisingly sympathetic.

—D.H.

Now at Local Theaters

Runelight and Moses—The new musical divinely inspired by *The Ten Commandments*. Fun-filled Biblical entertainment for the entire family. (Hit songs: "I Talk to the Bush" and "Take These Tablets and Call Me Tomorrow.")

The Man Who Could Be Wing—Gripping espionage thriller set in Shanghai.

Brute and Ranch—Musical based on TV's *Dallas*. Stars Tom Hanks in the singing role of J.R.

The Moaning of a Clan—Scary B-movie about a Scottish castle haunted by poltergeists.

Soilers of the Tea—A key event of the American Revolution supplies the theme for this dramatic new play.

The Sprite of Ring—The fantasy novels of J.R.R. Tolkien inspired a recently rediscovered Stravinsky ballet.

This Merely Was Nine—Documentary that takes a scathing view of the U.S. Supreme Court.

The Greatest Tory Ever Sold—Was Benedict Arnold guilty as charged?

The Beastie of the Bell—Musical version of *The Hunchback of Notre Dame* (libretto by Norman Mailer and Jack Henry Abbott).

—D.H.

In *The New York Times Magazine,* veteran puzzler Ivan Morris joined the game by suggesting *The Shaming of the True* and *The Folly of Praise.* Here are some other contributions to the genre:

Minnie's angry memoir: *Diary of a Had Mousewife.*
—Mark Lawrence, New York, N.Y., in The *New York* Magazine Competition

Tennessee Williams's play about an unpleasant dining experience: *The Salad of the Bad Cafe.*
—Silas Spitzer (at the time food editor of *Holiday* magazine), in *Saturday Review*

Thriller about an actress pursued by obsessed fan: *A Wish Called Fonda*.

> —Uncredited entry, The *New York* Magazine Competition

Each week, a neighborhood butcher is grilled by a panel of investigative journalists. Tune in for *Press the Meat*.

> —Source Unknown

Webitched! New version of the popular 1960s supernatural sitcom about the bickering Stevens family.

> —Christopher M. Hill, Troy, Mich., in "The Next Trend," the *Advertising Age* Magazine Competition

(The above is a nice example of an internal single-word transposition. The pun is also cited by Kermit Schafer as a blooper on an early children's radio program.)

And our final entertainment listing for the week:

She Conks to Stupor—A revolt by frustrated suburban homemakers provides the plot for this low-budget horror flick. Roseanne Barr, Eva Gabor, Betty White.

A footnote: I thought I had invented this one. Indeed, at the age of fifteen, I submitted it to the literary weekly *Saturday Review,* where it was published and credited to me. But my research for the present volume turned up a number of antecedents, including one in a book published in 1925. Of course, the Oliver Goldsmith stage play that inspired the pun has been around since 1773, so there's been plenty of time for clever people to "discover" the twist independently. It all confirms how thorny the problem of crediting originators can be.

Advertising

Puns are a favorite device of Madison Avenue copywriters. So it's hardly surprising that transpositions occasionally show up in magazine ads and commercials.

An ad contrasting a new Volvo with a pile of rusting competitive autos was headlined: "The earth shall inherit the weak." A poster for Scotch: "Teacher's is the greatest experience." Headline over an impressive photo of Waterford crystal decanters: "When it pours, it reigns." For wristwatches during the holiday season: "There is no present like the time."

An ad directed at travelers is headed: "Cities without a Stouffer hotel may be nice places to live, but you wouldn't want to visit there."

Those with long memories of pre-*perestroika* days may recall the Miller Lite commercial in which expatriate comedian Yakov Smirnoff confided: "In America, you can always find a party. In Russia, Party always find you."

Metropolitan Diary, an anecdotal weekly column in *The New York Times,* drew a contribution from Ellen Feld, who spotted this sign in the window of a Cincinnati sporting goods store (perhaps owned by a former actor): "Now is the discount of our winter tents."

In England, a familiar cry of ice cream vendors is "Stop me and buy one." It was wittily transformed into a slogan for a contraceptive: "Buy me and stop one."

But wait! Could advertisers be overlooking some terrific opportunities?

"My Beer, bist du Schön" would make a serviceable jingle for Michelob. (Credited to James Davis in a Bennett Cerf pun anthology.)

In a letter to *The Wall Street Journal,* Gary W. Emery of Bloomington, Indiana, noting an article about a new running shoe with a built-in computer to record speed and distance, suggests an appropriate slogan: "These are the soles that time men's tries." (The pun, if not the technology, was anticipated two decades earlier by Trudy Drucker in *Saturday Review.*)

As a freelance advertising copywriter, I am not unacquainted with headlines and slogans. Ergo, here are a few of my own nominations:

"It's enough to make your kin scrawl!"—Commercial for Crayola.

"For that earning and bitching sensation"—Recruiter targeting dissatisfied executives.

"Get your gas in 'ere!"—Hard-sell campaign for Mobil service stations.

"You gotta give a hammock"—L.L. Bean Christmas musical theme by Stephen Sondheim.

Two products for farmers: "Sup o' Coop," the gourmet chicken feed endorsed by Frank Perdue, and "Weed 'Em and Reap!," the new strain of fast-growing tomato seeds.

In a *Tonight Show* monologue, Jay Leno gave a fresh twist to a familiar campaign. "Mike Tyson was supposed to be in this new Coca-Cola commercial. But because of his loss to Buster Douglas, they had to change the slogan from 'Can't beat the feeling' to 'Can't feel the beating.' "

The Spoonerism Songbook

And now for some lyrical titles I'd like to see:

Kazoo players' love song: "You'd Be So Nice to Hum Comb to."

Torchy jazz lament about media coverage during a natural disaster: "News in the Blight."

Paul Simon's musical tribute to Archimedes: "Fifty Ways to Love Your Lever."

Caviar fisherman's refrain: "Boat, Boat, Boat Your Roe."

CHAPTER
4
Waste Is a Terrible Thing to Mind

A Spooneristic News Report

"It is the West of times; it is the burst of times!"

Scoff if you will, but transposition puns can shed light on current issues, illuminating the meaning behind events.

Perhaps this is why journalists are occasionally inspired to call upon them. For example:

An AP wire report about foreign currency exchange rates referred to traders "beating the pound." A BBC story on the convictions of mobsters described "mafia rats weaving raffia mats." And a *New York* magazine political column was headlined "Dame Luck Smiles on the Lame Duck."

Remember the famous garbage barge that cruised for months without finding a port that would allow it to dock? It only proved, said more than one wit, that waste is a terrible thing to mind.

In 1980, after a presidential candidate and his wife reportedly cried in public, a commentator admonished: "Hush, you Muskies!"

From the venerable *Wall Street Journal:*

An op-ed piece critical of arms negotiations by the Secretary of State is headlined "Baker Snatches Defeat from the Jaws of Victory." Playing off a popular film, an editorial about Craig Fields, a dismissed Pentagon official, is titled "Dreams of Fields." And a front-page story reports that after the mysterious disappearance of an Alabama businessman, his wife terminated financial support of her stepsons, resulting in "piqued twins."

The New York Times is also a fertile source of transposition punnery.

An article about a police crackdown on sidewalk vendors observes that "curbs on peddlers do not necessarily keep peddlers off curbs." A proposed $5 billion supercollider that would study atomic particles represents "the dreams of which stuff is made." A business analysis of the $1.6 billion deodorant industry is headlined "The Success of Sweet Smell." A review of a historical biography is titled "A Chance for America to Discover Columbus." Veteran bridge writer Alan Truscott heads a column "Kick That Block!"

Waxing nostalgic about the era of the great ocean liners, lately fallen upon harder days, a *Times* editorialist grumbles: "Some ships of state. Some state of ships." In other travel news, the Orient Express, notes a European dispatch, is called "the king of trains and the train of kings."

On fears that a proposed estate tax increase might motivate the wealthy to move elsewhere: "Many New Yorkers routinely say they are dying to leave the city. But will others now be leaving to die?"

In his columns, political commentator and language expert William Safire is partial to puns in general and transpositions on occasion. Here are three examples from three presidential administrations:

"Reagan fiddles while [Arthur] Burns roams" was a

typically sharp barb in a column on the economy. During the Carter years, Safire reported that the President ran across the White House lawn late one night to confront a group of demonstrators. Headline: "Through the Dark, Glassily." (Also apocryphally attributed to Dr. Spooner.) When Safire was a speechwriter in the Nixon White House, military officials in Vietnam failed to locate a hidden stock of weapons. An administration lawyer, the columnist claims, walked into his office and inquired: "Can you check a cache?"

In the Metropolitan Diary column of the *Times,* reader David Galef reported passing a Manhattan bank displaying a sign reading: "Your koala bear is unsafe and is being recalled by the manufacturer. . . . Please return your bear to us and choose another gift." Someone had taped a note to the window: "Beware of banks bearing free gifts." Mr. Galef penned his own addendum: "Beware of banks gifting free bears."

From a potpourri of other publications and sources:

A nostalgic piece about autumn by a *Louisville Courier-Journal* writer was titled "In Every Life a Little Fall Must Reign."

Opined *People* magazine in 1978, after that poorly translated presidential speech: "Amy Carter was poling the snows while daddy was snowing the Poles."

The birth of quintuplets inspired *Saturday Review* reader Allan R. Bosworth to speculate about the father's reaction after wading through hundreds of congratulatory letters and telegrams: "I seem to have sold my birthrate for a pot of messages." (As an apocryphal blooper, this Biblical pun dates from Spooner's time, at least.)

Saturday Review also defined "isolationist Democrats who switch views before election time" as "sheep in wolves' clothing."

In an installment of Randall Hylkema's acerbic cartoon strip in *Reason* magazine, a tiny grocery faces prosecution by antitrust regulators. "But we're just a little market on the corner!" protest Mom and Pop. "Maybe so," respond the feds, "but you've got a corner on the market."

Johnny Carson's observations on the news sometimes employ transpositions. Referring to then California State Comptroller Mike Curb, the *Tonight Show* host referred to a persistent reporter "dogging his Curb." And during a seafood contamination scare, Carson claimed that he drove his car off a pier and found tuna in his Mercury.

Some stories are too good to be true (or too true to be good). Despite painstaking research, I was unable to verify the following apocryphal tale:

When Onassis visited Beverly Hills to purchase a residence, he considered a mansion once owned by Mr. Keaton, the silent-film star. A newspaper photo caption supposedly read: "Aristotle Contemplating the Home of Buster."

Now here are some news items that I have personally unearthed with some assiduous investigative reporting:

Westchester, N.Y.—A strict antismoking ordinance was passed today. Town officials say their decision was influenced by thousands of signatures on a citizens' petition that began "Ours is not to wheeze in Rye . . ."

Silicon Valley, Calif.—The NCR Corporation today announced a revolutionary new product: a Local Area Network that requires no cabling. The wireless system instead transmits computer data via radio waves. Commented a company engineer: "I never met a LAN I didn't mike."

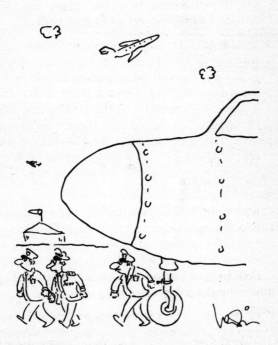

O'Hare Airport, Chicago—A commercial pilot recklessly boasted that he was smuggling narcotics in the fuselage of his plane. The conversation was overheard by nearby federal agents. He was immediately arrested for stuffing his strut and strutting his stuff.

New York, N.Y.—Imelda Marcos was released from prison today, after posting bond sufficient to meet a court ruling. "Looks like we got her ass out of the slammer," said Gerry Spence, Mrs. Marcos's flamboyant, plain-spoken Wyoming lawyer. When asked how his client felt, Spence shouted: "Bright-eyed and tushy-bailed!"

Washington, D.C.—A spokesman for the U.S. Mint today announced that a new fifty-cent commemorative coin would be issued to honor two great American patriots. On one side is the face of Theodore Roosevelt; on the reverse the likeness of Nathan Hale. Asked why these two historic figures had been selected for the same coin, the official replied: "This way, whenever people need to make a decision with a coin toss, they can simply call 'Teds or Hales?' "

New York, N.Y.—Owen Laster, head of worldwide literary operations for the William Morris Agency, has been named exclusive representative of the estate of the late Sylvia Plath, best known for *The Bell Jar*. The partnership thus constructed will be known as Laster and Plath.

Elkhart, Ind.—A recessionary climate is creating excess inventories, according to recently released government statistics. A local manufacturer confirmed the accuracy of the reports first-hand today as he gloomily surveyed his overflowing warehouse. Turning to his foreman, he barked: "Take this stuff and job it!"

Princeton, N.J.—The most expensive of the University's elite "eating clubs" levies an annual membership fee of $4,500. Because Princeton's tuition is $16,570 a year, a college education might be described as "27% frat fee."

And speaking of waste being a terrible thing to mind, let us conclude our review of the news with this report:

On a PBS documentary, a University of Arizona professor explained that "the idea of archeology is to learn about past civilizations by looking at ancient garbage." It just confirms the truth of that famous principle: "Mess is lore."

CHAPTER
5
Nothing to Choose but Your Lanes

Improbable Definitions and Unlikely Quotations

As Shakespeare said, brevity is the soul of wit. (As James Brown said, it's the wit of soul.) The pithiest transposition puns are often the most effective. Consider these brief definitions, explications, and elaborations from our Spooneristic Encyclopedia:

Alimony: (1) *The ties of exes are upon you.* (2) *The bounty of mutiny.*
    —(1) Howard Gossage; (2) Source Unknown

Research psychologists: *Pulling habits out of rats.*
—George P. Schmidt, quoted in *Saturday Review*

Botanical discovery: *A new lice on leaf.*
        —Ed Horr, quoted in *Saturday Review*

Truckers: *De bigger dey are, de farder dey haul.*
            —Source Unknown

Eloping coed: *She put the heart before the course.*
    —George S. Kaufman (*Alternative definitions:*
        Predinner romance; Eschewing golf in
        deference to one's spouse.)

Declining blue-collar support for the Democratic
Party: *Labor's Love Lost.*
        —Victor H. Bernstein, New Milford, Conn.,
            in a letter to *The New York Times*

Problems created by longer male hairstyles: *A
man's comb is his hassle.*
        —Gary Moore, New York, N.Y. (and others)
            in The *New York* Magazine Competition

Counterfeiters: *They earn money the hard way—
they make it.*
        —Elizabeth Critas, Cincinnati, Ohio,
            in The *New York* Magazine Competition

Children sharing toys: *The din of inequity.*
        —*The Complete Pun Book,* by Art. Moger

Racetracks: *Where windows clean people.*
                    —*Mad* Magazine

Champagne: *Sips that passion the night.*
                    —Source Unknown

Venue for jogging clergymen: *God and Run Club.*
                    —Source Unknown

Consequence of infectious disease: *Murder of an
Anatomy.*
                    —*Mad* Magazine

Combined charity drive: *Putting all your begs in one ask-it.*

> —Clifton Fadiman (Contrast the above phonemic transposition with the syllabic "Don't put all your Basques in one exit," page 48).

The eerie feeling that you never want to be in this place again: *Vujà dé.*

> —Washington Novelist Sally Quinn, quoted by William Safire

And here are a few of my own one-line contributions:

Miscasting *Benji* movies: *Square pegs in hound roles.*

Unpopular baseball team: *Mitts and Hisses.*

Occupational hazard plaguing striptease dancers who perform at stag parties: *Icing on the slip.*

Aphrodisiac formulated by Friedrich Nietzsche: *The Pill to Wow 'Er.*

Elevator music: *Canned and bore us.*

How trolley enthusiasts describe their passion: *A Desire Named Streetcar.*

Vegetarian's eulogy for a chicken salad: *Or I'll Mourn You in Dressing.*

Why boxers should be punctual: *They're weighing-in late for him.*

Country bumpkin who falls for TV pitches selling cheap Zirconium jewelry: *Cubic's rube.*

Maxim for overstressed computer trainers: *It is better to use a cursor than to curse a user.*

What's wrong with the defense industry: *Poor workers and war perkers.*

Euclid's lost principle of squaring the circle: *First sum, first curved.*

Hotheaded Ku Klux Klan members: *They burn their crosses as soon as they're bridged.*

Manufacturer of fencing guaranteed to keep out dogs (an equal opportunity employer): *Gates and Strays.*

Fertilized ovum: *The thing of shapes to come.*

Postpartum depression: *The Blues of the Birth.*

During his abortive 1964 election campaign, TV critic and humorist Marvin Kitman opined: "I'd rather be president than write." And what might Gunther Gebel-Williams say about lion taming? "It never pains but it roars."

Here are some of my own contributions for *Bartlett's Unfamiliar Quotations:*

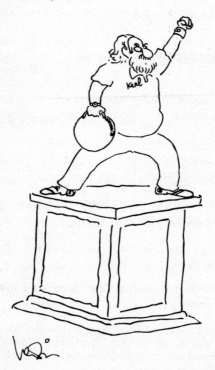

Karl Marx's position on indoor sports: "Bowlers of the world, arise; you have nothing to choose but your lanes!"

Marcel Marceau, with characteristic humility: "It's only a tatter of mime."

Henry Luce on the eve of the Chicago fire: "There'll be a hot town in the old *Time* tonight."

Mark Twain on high-wire performers: "Everyone walks about the tether . . ."

Daedalus's resigned comment on Icarus, after their ill-fated flight: "No sooner dead than son."

Oncologist's exclamation upon consuming a potent alcoholic beverage: "That really whacks a polyp!"

Why Colonel Sanders was so finicky: "Who knows what evil lurks in the marts of hen?"

Farmer to traveling salesman: "You're weddin' the daughter, or you're dead in the water!"

Even *names* of well-known personalities can be fancifully redefined. Here are my nominees for a spooneristic *Who's Who:*

Dairy heiress who uses her fortune to construct a time machine that transports her back to the Civil War: *Butter Queen McFly.*

Octogenarian sadomasochist: *Whip van Wrinkle.*

Football coach unable to work due to a congenital injury, but who nevertheless cheers enthusiastically for his team: *Root Knock-knee.*

Entrepreneur who funds antiwar causes: *Peace Ralley.*

Jazz musician and animal rights advocate: *Charlie "Purred" Barker.*

Defeated general: *Custer Beaten.*

Baseball player continually on the sidelines: *Waived Infield.*

News most dreaded by aspiring late-night TV talk-show hosts: *Carson Gainin'.*

Finally, this classic conundrum, of unknown origin: What's the difference between a rooster and a lawyer? The rooster wakes up in the morning and clucks defiance. (No letters, please!)

CHAPTER
6
Every Day Has Its Dog
"Spoonericks" and
Other Verse Cases

Spoonerick is a portmanteau word I created to describe a limerick with a transposition pun ending. The following examples appeared in The *New York* Magazine Competition. The first six compositions won prizes.

A man who made mats met an adder
In his shop, at the top of a ladder.
   And in spite of his knack
   For biting right back
Can no longer be had as a matter.

       —Brian Shay, New York, N.Y.

The crooner loved golf with such might
He'd practice 'ere dawn's early light.
   Making neighbors so nervous
   They cried "Saints preserve us
From Bings that go thump in the night."

       —Fred Raymond, Dunedin, Fla.

The anatomy lecturer said
To the students enrolled in premed:

If you feel it's too shoddy
To study the body,
You may go to the class of the head.

—Mary Diamond,
Glen Gardner, N.J.

Said Joe Namath's surgeon, "I bridle,
And feel, let me say, homicidal,
Right now and in future
When threading a suture
To go through the knee of an idol."

—Albert G. Miller, New York, N.Y.

(The above transposition—sans football and verse
—was among those spuriously attributed to Spooner.
A Mr. Charles W. Baty confessed that he perpetrated
it at Oxford in 1920.)

He was hired by A. Tel & Tel.
His credentials seemed perfectly swell.
But an envious crony
Exposed him as phone-y.
(He was tossed like a hat out of Bell.)

—Rosemarie Williamson,
Basking Ridge, N.J.

Said Fidel to some girls in bandanas:
"I smoke so I won't go bananas.
Now my craving's acute,
May I light this cheroot?"
Said the girls: "Yes, we ban no Havanas."

—Albert G. Miller, New York, N.Y.

A passionate cook from Saipan
By his head chef was given the can.
    "Your baking is fine,
    But we must draw the line
At indulging your pash in the flan."
                —L.J.T. Biese, Hill, N.H.

A lissome young miss was in tears,
The butt of lewd whistles and jeers.
    She stood it awhile,
    Then said with a smile:
"Countrymen, end me your leers."
                —Sunny Kramer, Harrison, N.Y.

Young Hamlet said, "Far from sublime,
The food at this inn is a crime.
    For the flavor at hand
    Is exceedingly bland,
And I find that the joint's out of thyme."
                —Dana T. Ring, West Hartford, Conn.

(Shorn of the clever verse, the above pun was
credited to Marcia Ringel in *Saturday Review* several
decades ago.)

When Dorothy strolled through the park
She decided to swim (on a lark).
    And so she dove in,
    Then she spotted a fin.
And now there's a Dot in the shark.
                —Unsigned entry

Poor Susan, you're really undone.
You tell me that now you've begun

To think that the Sister
Is hiding your mister?
There's nothing, Sue, under the nun!

—Marjorie B. Friedman, Buffalo, N.Y.

Said Oxford's old Earl, "I can't sleep!
O'er Shakespeare's demands I could weep!
  May Judith betray him,
  'Twould break me to pay him
That dowry; Will's daughters run steep!"

—John Hines, Rio Piedras, Puerto Rico

Yul Brynner said: "Now I admit
I'm flabby because I just sit."
  He's back in a play,
  His physique is okay.
He had to be Thai'd to be fit.

—Dr. Arnold Diamond,
Bay Terrace, N.Y.

There once was a ghoul, brokenhearted.
From his pals, evil glances were darted.
  They steered clear of his way,
  Causing wise men to say
That a ghoul and his fold are soon parted.

—Miles Klein, East Brunswick, N.J.
(also, in earlier variants, Clark
Smith, Baltimore, and Judith M.
Kass, New York, N.Y.)

Here are three spoonericks of my own:

The minister patiently grins
At rude noise when his sermon begins.
　For loud oafs he corrects
　By the text he selects.
It's the passage: "Christ sighed for our dins."

Odysseus was struck by a curse, see,
Which left his men pleading for mercy.
　To beasts they were changed;
　Each visage rearranged.
(You might call them The Misters of Circe.)

A New England schoolgirl named Finn
Panned for gold; often scored a big win.
　But she called it all quits
　For her parents had fits
'Cause their daughter was sieving in Lynn.

Besides Spoonericks, other verse forms neatly accommodate transpositions. Consider these examples:

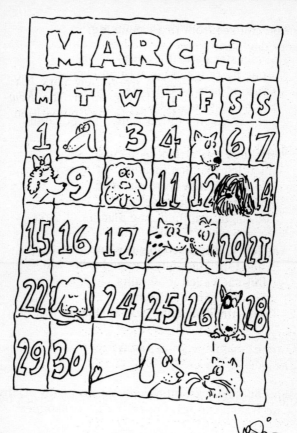

Monday's dog is fair of face;
Tuesday's dog is full of grace.
Wednesday's dog never sheds;
Thursday's dog sleeps on beds.
Friday's dog always drools;
Saturday's and Sunday's need obedience schools.

As you can see from this canine log,
Every day has its dog.

> —Lydia Wilen, New York, N.Y.
> a prizewinner in The *New
> York* Magazine Competition

Reflection on Watching Nureyev Dance:

> The best I do is plod
> while he leaps high—
> There but for the god
> of grace go I.

> —Leo Freilich, Metropolitan Diary,
> *The New York Times*

> Did Hilaire Belloc live
> on a Bel Air hillock?

—Carol Ehrsam, Metropolitan Diary,
The New York Times

And here's my own brief eulogy for a pet struck by
a car:

> Run over.
> Un-Rover.

Transpositions lend themselves naturally to verse because a phonemic transposition, paired with the origi-

nal, creates a rhyme. More spooneristic poetry may be found in the following chapters. A German transpositional verse form is called *Schüttelreim,* examples of which begin on page 131.

CHAPTER
7
It's Bound to Be Fun, and . . .

Sexual Spoonerisms

(CAUTION! You must be over eighteen to be
admitted to this chapter.)

If you like erotic humor (or even if you're just a pheas-
ant plucker), this is your ducky lay!

Virtually every form of humor has its sexual aspect.
Transposition puns are no exception. As language experts point out, English is so loaded with multiple
meanings that almost *any* innocent remark can result
in a *double entendre.*

"Spoonerisms play a major role in the formation of
bawdy jokes," observes Richard Lederer in *Maledicta,*
a scholarly journal devoted entirely to vulgarity and
general naughtiness. (Best-selling punster Lederer, at
the time a teacher at a conservative boarding school,
prudently penned this piece under a pseudonym.) For
sexually explicit transpositions, he coined the evoca-
tive term *poonerism.*

Some vintage specimens of this genre might today
be construed as sexist or otherwise offensive. They

often take the classic "difference between" form (see page 25). For instance:

> What's the difference between a tribe of pygmies and a girls' track team? The first is a bunch of cunning runts . . .

> What's the difference between a chorus girl [or boardinghouse owner or chambermaid, etc.] during the day and at night? By day she is fair and buxom, but at night . . .

Gershon Legman, probably the leading authority on erotic folklore and humor, has archived expressions that take an unexpectedly graphic turn when transposed: "snatch a kiss," "a soul full of hope," and the rather bizarre parody lyric in which a distractingly beautiful woman "forces Pushkin (from your mind)."

Another example cited by Legman, though imperfect as a transposition, is nevertheless interesting in its permutations: "the mock book-title *Memoirs of a Milkmaid, or Forty Years of Scum-Creaming*, I mean *Scream Coming*, I mean *Cream Skimming* . . ."

So whatever your way of life or lay of wife, whether you are in the throes of passion or a pose of thrashin', always remember that it's smarter to cop a feel than to feel a cop. And of course, shun the penny-ante in favor of any panty.

Where else but *Playboy* would you turn for sexual humor? Here, from the magazine's back-of-the-centerfold joke page, is a potpourri of spooneristic jokes:

The pop music groupie found her idol outside the theater and was soon between a hard and a rock place.

Have you heard about the up-and-coming porno film actor whose rise is starring?

A dedicated prostitute refused to be sidelined by a case of Rocky Mountain spotted fever. She took a ticking, but she kept on licking.

Then there was the pimp with so many girls on his payroll that he was up to his alligators in ass.

Remember when Procter & Gamble learned about Marilyn Chambers's porno film appearance and promptly pulled the model's face from their detergent packages? Now her picture isn't on boxes because her box is in pictures.

Downscale soap opera: *The Lays of Our Dives.*

If Dr. Spooner were still around, he might officiate at a wedding with the words: "If anyone present knows why this couple should not be joyfully loined together . . ."

Of course, the groom on that occasion was an old-fashioned young fellow who nervously blurted to his girlfriend's father: "Sir, I am asking for your daughter's hole in handy matrimony."

What's the difference between an alarm clock and a penis? One goes off to get a guy up, while the other goes up to get a guy off.

It was the secretary's first day on the new job. When her roommate asked what happened, she replied: "First I was introduced to one of the members of the firm. Then I was introduced to the firm of one of the members."

A golfer remarked to his buddy on the obvious charms of the attractive new member. "Forget it," advised the friend. "She's an unpliable lay."

Why don't pimps attend night school? Because they would rather book the cracks than crack the books.

"Bumper crops this season," the rural madam approvingly told the members of her staff as cash-laden farmers began appearing. "So," replied one of the girls, "it's time once again for the harvest-boon maul."

A college student was arrested for mooning through a closed dormitory window. The charge: being an ass in the pane.

Playboy's Unabashed Dictionary defines: _bordello_ as a toll-cookie house . . . _obese hooker_ as a roly holer . . . _quickie_ as gunning the jump . . . _hot tub_ as a balling bowl . . . and _shipboard procurer_ as a snatch purser.

In "Little Annie Fanny," the _Playboy_ comic strip created by Harvey Kurtzman and Will Elder, a jock with two glamorous females clutching his body inspires the envious comment: "Look at the dolls on that boob!"

Also appearing in *Playboy* was an article on a retail chain called Pleasure Chest, which sells a wide variety of, er . . . unusual and creative bondage devices. Journalist D. Keith Mano wryly observed: "They're almost in restraint of trade in trade of restraint."

In Chapter 1, we presented Kermit Schafer's radio and TV bloopers. Some were too explicit to include until this chapter. Now they can be told:

A bakery commercial offered listeners "the breast in bed."

The classic Dickens novel became *"A Sale of Two Titties."*

On an educational TV program, a "film strip" turned into a "strip film."

The appearance of a head of state was preceded by this announcement: "It gives me great pleasure to introduce you to the Virgin of Governor's Island."

This flub proved so incisive that it is still quoted on T-shirts and other venues for profundity: "Our next record is dedicated to all you gals who don't appreciate us men enough. A hard man is good to find."

Station identification: "This is the Dominion Network of the Canadian Broadcorping Castration."

And another station break: "This is KTIW, Sexas Titty—uh, Texas City."

A disc jockey introduced an Andy Williams song as "Can't Get Loose to Using You."

Performing in *The Merchant of Venice,* an actor gave unintended new meaning to Shakespeare when he accidentally transposed Shylock's line "Shall I lay perjury upon my soul?"

In *Verbatim,* Norman Ward tells of a radio announcer who identified the Pig and Whistle, a sponsoring restaurant, as the "Piss and Wiggle."

Here are a few of my own contributions to the dubious craft of erotic transposition punnery:

You are invited to an S&M party. It's bound to be fun. (And fun to be bound!)

What's a rookie patrolman's first task? Meeting his beat.

A woman of insatiable sexual appetites eagerly headed for a town in Vermont. Was she disappointed! On arrival, she discovered that it's really called Bellows Falls.

Slogan for an impotence remedy: "It's help to get good hard."

Scandal on *Sesame Street*! Ms. Piggy decided to try prostitution, but found it tough to recruit many customers. She confesses the whole sad story in her torchy musical lament "It Isn't Green Being Easy."

If the verse in the previous chapter was not enough, here are a few sexual spoonericks and other prurient poetry:

> "They have no head for figures," he said,
> "So my girls keep the firm in the red.
>   But I don't fret or frown,
>   Since they love to go down,
> And they sure have the figures for head!"
>
> —*Playboy*

> Young Raymond was careless, they say,
> In planning his rolls in the hay;
>   For his last bedded doll

Was a Mob *capo*'s moll.
The results was: Some holes in the Ray!

—*Playboy*

She offered her honor;
He honored her offer.
And all night long,
It was on her and off her.

—Antique graffito cited in the
New York *Village Voice*

Sex Over 40: Mature or Premature?

When you were young, you might have said:
"I am the master of my fate."

But now you might remark in bed:
"I am the faster of my mate."

—D.H.

Finally, these sexy spoonerisms from various sources:

A Benny Hill skit: "I'll tickle it if you wash it . . . Uh, I mean, I'll *tackle* it if you *wish* it."

Jeff Greenfield in the *Village Voice,* speculating on Martina Navratilova's sexual experiences: "The male is in the Czech."

Seduction in the pantry, or "Your cook is goosed!" (Sometimes cited as an early radio blooper.)

Maledicta quoted the hooker's cordial farewell: "It's been a business doing pleasure with you."

Well, I'm tempted to offer more sexual puns, but this looks like a good place to quit. After all, you can't get stud from a blown! (Or is it the other way around?)

Before we end this chapter, however, "The Two Ronnies" (see page 116) have supplied us with this late news flash:

For making improper remarks to Shirley Bassey, Shirley Maclaine, and Shirley Temple Black, a man was given a lengthy prison term. At his sentencing he cried: "They got me by the court and Shirleys!"

CHAPTER
8
Nosy Cooks and Lirty Dies

Works of Multiple
Transposition Punnery

So far, we have seen only the most basic forms of spooneristic humor: short stories and one-line jokes with single (occasionally double) transposition-pun punch lines.

But the true mastery of the craft is the "extended" work: the tour-de-force opus containing *multiple* transpositions.

At public appearances, Richard Lederer recites a spoonerized fairy tale, "Prinderella and the Cince." The routine was created by the early radio comedian "Colonel Stoopnagle" (Frederick Chase Taylor), who often made use of transposition puns and who similarly fractured several other fables and nursery rhymes. (The monologue, mostly nonsense, appears in Lederer's *Get Thee to a Punnery*.)

Contributors to *Word Ways*, "the journal of recreational linguistics," have submitted compositions of this genre. For example, Britisher J. A. Lindon devised a conversation about the weather in a language he dubbed "Spoonerian." An excerpt: "Blocking showy, Miss Thorning." ("Shocking blowy this morning.")

For a while, *Word Ways* readers vied to top each

other with multiple-pun "Spoonerhymes." This sample, entitled "Family Picnic in Milwaukee" is by Mary J. Hazard: "Beer nigh?/Nearby./In casks?/Kin asks."

Here are some dazzling displays of pyrotechnic punnery:

The Capitol Steps Presents
Lirty Dies

The Capitol Steps is a Washington-based musical-political satire troupe. Although most of their repertoire consists of parodies of popular songs, this ingenious (non-musical) monologue generates the most enthusiastic audience response.

Not every reversal makes sense (or even forms legitimate words), but the overall effect is nevertheless amusing, especially when performed in the deadpan style of Bill Strauss, who cowrote it with Elaina Newport.

The text is frequently updated to include the most current gossip. On one occasion, it was even translated into sign language for a hearing-impaired audience.

There is nothing worse than a vicious scandal. Let me say that again: There is wothing nurse than a scicious vandal.

First, the Me-T-L pinistry of Bammy Taker and her jusband, Him. These pre-vee teachers findled their swallowers. They mollected killions, then masted the wunny on thidiculous rings like a dancy foghouse. While Bammy went on tropping ships, Ferry Jalwell said Him was a hoset clomosexual. They were in trig bubble. Now, Bammy and Him are tack on the boob. Him says he has my horals. What a lirty die! If they're such fell swellas, how come Hessica Jahn is plosing for *Payboy*? Now that's a shirty dame!

My stekond sory is about Ronna Dice and her froy bend, Harry Gart. Ronna was a lung yovely in a popless tose. Harry was a fiddle-aged mella, and a Juan Don. Harry wasn't wearing his bedding wand and Ronna got a himpse of his gland. So they bopped ahoard the Bunkey Misness and sook tail. Someone fook a toto of Ronna litting on Harry's sap. What a rig bisk for Harry! Then, nate one light, Ronna went to Harry's hown-touse for some panky-hanky. Outside, rooping sneporters saw the boo from the tushes. They stot the gory, and made cub-lic the population. Harry kickly qualled his life, Wee, and said he was a sponogamous mouse. What a lirty die! Harry thill stinks he can prun for resi-dent. Chat fance, Harry!

My stirred thory is about Kister Mennedy of Chassamoosits. The fater-pamilias of the Clennedy Kan. Kister Mennedy is a laming fliberal—and a gorny hi! He set-jetted to Balm Peach with a sephew and a nun. They went to a cly-hass clite-nub and chubble-dugged a few Warvey Ballhangers. Then Kister Mennedy said: "It's almost clore-o-fock. Let's go to my heach bouse for a little kite-nap!" The poo-snapers say Kister Mennedy went tie-hailing around the heach bouse wearing only a she-tirt. Kister Men-nedy thill stinks he can be a pantsy folitician on the sore of the Flenate. What a lirty die! He'd better keep his bowsers truckled!

The storal of these mories is this: If you tell a lirty die, you deceive what you reserve!

"Bass-Ackwards"

A Presidential Foray into Transpositional Humor

by Abraham Lincoln

Lincoln employed humor, biographers tell us, as a courtroom technique, as a political weapon, and as a way of coping with frequent bouts of depression.

Spooneristic humor was popular in the American

West, and it evidently fascinated Lincoln. A fellow attorney in Illinois recalled: "No one could ever use the word 'facsimile' in Lincoln's presence without his adding 'sick family.'" (Too bad Abe didn't live long enough to witness the proliferation of fax machines.)

The following composition has been identified simply as a "piece" which Lincoln wrote and handed to Arnold Robinson, the crier (bailiff) of the U.S. Circuit Court in Springfield. Although the manuscript is unquestionably in Lincoln's hand, not all historians are persuaded that it was his original creation.

In 1956, the editors of *Gentry* (a snazzy-but-now-defunct quarterly magazine) reproduced the essay with some fanfare, expressing surprise that an American president could display such an "earthy side." (Hmmm . . . they should hear The Capitol Steps's description, above, of more recent escapades involving politicians.)

He said he was riding *bass-ackwards* on a *jass-ack*, through a *patton-cotch*, on a pair of *baddle-sags*, stuffed full of *binger-gred*, when the animal *steered* at a *scump*, and the *lirrup-steather* broke, and throwed him in the *forner* of the *kense*, and broke his *pishing-fole*. He said he would not have minded it much, but he fell right in a great *tow-curd*; in fact, he said it give him a right smart *sick* of *fitness*—he had the *molera-corbus* pretty bad. He said, about *bray dake* he come to himself, ran home, seized up a *stick* of *wood*, and split the *axe* to make a light, rushed into the house, and found the *door* sick abed, and his *wife* standing open. But thank goodness she is getting right *hat* and *farty* again.

"The Two Ronnies"

Present

Dr. Spooner at the Teckfast Brable

In the 1970s, *The Two Ronnies,* a TV comedy program, entertained millions in the UK on the BBC, and in the US via PBS. (That's just my initial opinion.)

Ronnie Barker and Ronnie Corbett (one is the large one, and the other is the short one) particularly relished wordplay. Spoonerisms were a specialty.

A typical sketch might have a soldier denounced as a "sore little pod" because he forgot his "rusty trifle," thereby placing "Dave Granger in grave danger." Another might take place at a "shower flow," or a restaurant serving "chalk pops," or even in the home of a man being ordered to "heave your louse," despite the protestation that he is "bill instead."

It was inevitable that Spooner himself would one day receive a left-handed tribute. Writer Dick Vosburgh imagines a morning conversation between the Good Doctor (portrayed by Ronnie Barker) and his wife:

Mrs. S.   Ah, there you are, William. Beautiful day, isn't it?

Dr. S.   Quite so—the shine is sunning, the chirds are burping—lovers are killing and booing . . . it makes one glide to be a lav!

Mrs. S.   It's just as well you're in a good mood. *(She hands him a shirt)* Because look what the laundry did to your best shirt.

Dr. S.   Good Heavens. They've freed the slaves!

MRS. S. Frayed the sleeves, dear.

DR. S. I did that, saidn't I?

MRS. S. They've also torn the collar and smashed all the buttons.

DR. S. *(Looking closer)* Quite so! It never pains but it roars. Buttons, collar and sleeves at one swell foop! Well, I'll fight them nooth and tail! Naith and tool! I'll go down and smith them to smashereens. *(Goes toward the door)* I'm going to tump in a jaxi!

MRS. S. William—wait! Surely, such a scene would be unseemly for a man of your calling?

DR. S. *(Returning to table)* You're quite right, my dear. After all, I *am* a clan of the moth. Better to let sleeping logs die. To hue is ermine. *(He sits)*

MRS. S. That's better. Do you feel like some breakfast?

DR. S. Indood I dee! A suggestion to warm the hartles of my—cockles of my heart. I rather fancy some hot toatered bust, a rasher of strakey beacon, and some of that cereal that goes pap, snockle and crap.

MRS. S. Very well, William. And while you're eating it, I shall be packing my trunk.

DR. S. Tracking your punk?

MRS. S. Yes, William. You see, I'm leaving and I'm not coming back.

DR. S. Leaving me after twenty years of bedded wiss? This must be some rather jathetic poke. You can't mean suddenly to destroy my entire lay of wife!

MRS. S. I'm quite serious, William. I'm leaving and I'm not coming back.

DR. S. But my dear, consider the word of the

Highly Boble: "What God hath joined together, let no sun put Amanda." Er . . . "Let no pan soot amunder" . . . Dear me, I'm getting my tang all tungled!

MRS. S. Exactly. That's why I'm leaving you.

DR. S. What do you mean?

MRS. S. It's quite simple, William. I can't spoon any more Standerisms!

Not quite. Although Mrs. Spooner often looked askance at her husband's eccentricities, the couple remained happily married for fifty-two years.

In his 1988 autobiography, *It's Hello from Him!,* Ronnie Barker recalls: "I loved doing Spoonerisms but they were swine [real tough!] to master. . . . The trouble is . . . the subconscious automatically puts things right—Spoonerising the Spoonerism! . . . When it flows, though, it's glorious."

Twist-Rime on Spring
by Arthur Guiterman

My father loved the light verse of the late Arthur Guiterman. A popular poet decades ago, Guiterman is, sadly, not so well known today. From his book *The Light Guitar,* published in 1923, here is a pastoral celebration in spooneristic couplets:

Upon the hills new grass is seen;
The vender's garden sass is green.

The birds between the showers fly;
The woods are full of flowers shy.

The ornamental butterfly
Expands his wings to flutter by.

The bees, those little honey-bugs,
Are gayly dancing bunny hugs,

While poets sing in tripping rime
That Spring's a simply ripping time!

Winter Eve
by Robert Morse

This introspective monologue is a clever tour de force of transpositions. All the words are real, although the net effect is mostly nonsense. The title itself is a transposition (of "interweave"). The irreverent fourth line from the end is especially interesting; it might be called a spooneristic *tmesis:* the intercutting of one transposition pun within another.

Drear fiend: How shall this spay be dent?
I jell you toque—I do not know.
What shall I do but snatch the woe
that falls beneath my pane, and blench
my crows and ted my briny shears?
Now galls another class. I'll sit
and eye the corn that's fought in it.
Maces will I fake, and heart my pare.
Is this that sold elf that once I was
with lapped chips and tolling lung?
I hollow sward and tight my bung
for very shame, and yet no cause—
save that the beery witchery
of Life stows grail. Shall I abroad?

Track up my punks? Oh gray to pod
for him who sanders on the wee!
I'll buff a stag with shiny torts
and soulful hocks, a truthbush too,
perhaps a rook to bead—but no!
my wishes must be dashed. Reports
of danger shake the reaming scare.
Whack against blight! Against that tune,
"A gritty pearl is just like a titty prune"
blows from the fox. I cannot bear
this sweetness. Silence is best. I mat
my mistress and my sleazy lumber.
I'll shake off my toes, for they encumber.
What if I tub my stow? The newt
goes better faked to the cot.
I'll hash my wands or shake a tower,
(a rug of slum? a whiskey sour?)
water my pants in all their plots,
slob a male hairy before I seep—
and dropping each id on heavy lie,
with none to sing me lullaby,
slop off to dreep, slop off to dreep.

The Cozy Nook Trio

by Ira Gershwin

The Firebrand of Florence was a 1945 Broadway musical with music by Kurt Weill and lyrics by Ira Gershwin.

Four years earlier, Weill and Gershwin's *Lady in the Dark* was a big hit. But *Firebrand* was plagued by creative and production problems, and was to be their last collaboration. Following mixed reviews, it closed after just forty-three performances and today is almost forgotten.

Ira Gershwin loved wordplay. Among the songs he wrote for *Firebrand* is "The Cozy Nook Trio," which is built around inadvertent transposition puns in classic spoonerism style. (The title pun is often apocryphally attributed to Spooner.)

Firebrand was based on a successful 1924 play about the Renaissance artist Benvenuto Cellini. Gershwin sets the scene for us:

"The *palazzo* garden in moonlight. Duke Alessandro is making a play for Cellini's model, Angela. But his passes are fraught with apprehension, as he senses that Cellini lurks in the background. At times the sardonic latter sneaks a glance over the hedge."

DUKE:	Dear young woman, when I'm gazing
	Fondly at you, it's amazing
	How much love I'd like to vow.
	But though I've had a lot of practice
	At this sort of thing, the fact is
	I am not myself just now.
ANGELA:	Dear my lord, I feel you're scoffing.
DUKE:	With Cellini in the offing,
	I'm as nervous as can be.
ANGELA:	Your highness—
DUKE:	Call me Bumpy.
ANGELA:	You do seem rather jumpy.
DUKE:	I beg you bear with me.
	[Refrain:]
	I know where there's a nosy cook—
ANGELA:	My lord, you mean a cozy nook?
DUKE:	Yes, yes, of course! A cozy nook for two.
	And there we two can kill and boo.
ANGELA:	My lord, you mean we'll bill and coo?

CELLINI: It seems to me that killing and booing
            should do.

DUKE: I cannot promise bedding wells.

ANGELA: My thoughts were not on wedding bells.

DUKE: Whatever I do is for the fatherland;
                And so I love your sturgeon vile.

ANGELA: My lord, you mean my virgin style?

DUKE: It's wonderful how love can understand!
            Listen, loveliest of your gender:
            Somehow, phrases soft and tender
                Do not sound their best tonight.

ANGELA: It seems you get the words all twisted.

DUKE: But the way that you assisted
                Thrills me through with sheer delight.

ANGELA: When the ducal throat is vocal,
            Women from afar, or local,
                Always know what's on his mind.

CELLINI: The situation vexes;
            I'm finding out that sex is
                The curse of humankind.

DUKE: *[Refrain:]*
            I know where there's a booden wench—

ANGELA: My lord, you mean a wooden bench?

DUKE: Yes, yes, of course! A wooden bench for
            two.
                And there we two can biss a kit.

ANGELA: My lord, you mean we'll kiss a bit?

CELLINI: He may be biting more biss-a-kit than he
            can chew!

ANGELA: How masterf'ly you stress your puit!
                I mean the way you press your suit;
            I sense it from the way you press my
            hand.

DUKE: And so I offer wedless bliss.

ANGELA: I'd rather it were bedless wiss.
DUKE: It's wonderful how love can understand.

In his 1959 memoir, *Lyrics on Several Occasions,* Ira Gershwin alludes gracefully to the show's modest run:

"More than thirty years ago [1924], in *Lady, Be Good!,* I tried for a number based on spoonerisms, but it never made rehearsal. This later attempt, 'The Cozy Nook Trio,' was, I think, not unagreeably accepted by the few who paid to see *The Firebrand of Florence,* and by the few more who came in on passes."

So versatile is the transposition pun that it can be used to reconstruct entire works of literature in miniature. Consider my own modest submission (with apologies to Oscar Wilde):

". . . And Devil Take the Mind Host"
(A Short Gothic Novel)

I was a man without a choral mode. As a child, I was the shack bleep of the family. My parents often shouted: "You are a boiled sprat!"

Why did I commission that portrait? There it was, facing me in the stair. Insane plight! It was enough to make my kin scrawl. Frankly, I was shared skitless! I wanted to destroy it with my hair bands!

Sure, I was huggedly ransom. But the picture seemed to be saying: "I can bead you like a rook. You think you're awful pretty, but you're pretty awful. Once you were tough and ruthless, but soon you will be rough and toothless. I will hear no answer—just tight your bung."

After that scathing diatribe, I knew it was all over. I was damned with paint phrase!

The Frustrations of Suburban Gardening

(A column appearing in this space each Sunday)

Let's face it: The problems of weekend gardeners are hardly new.

As far back as Old Testament times, the Israelites found that tending to their fertile backyards was a tedious and boring chore. Thus the oft-heard observation: "He's just mowing through the Goshens."

Today, of course, lawn care supplies and services may be purchased with a credit card. No wonder the ads say: "Don't heave loam without it." Hank Thevins for that, anyway.

Don't neglect those common garden pests, especially if you discover a new lice on leaf. Dead trees must be expunged brute and ranch.

If you are slothful about these tasks, you will have to make up for tossed lime. But the diligent will weed 'em and reap!

—D.H.

CHAPTER
9
Le Père de Marie dans eine Hängematte

Transposition Puns Around the World

Transposition puns—both deliberate and accidental —occur in languages other than English.

In French, *contrepèterie* (a compound of "against" and "to make a sound") is a popular pastime. *Contrepets* often appear in *Le Canard Enchaîné,* the Paris-based satirical newspaper. A number of book-length compilations have been published in France. These transpositions are usually of the phonemic type.

Some simple examples: *Le père de Marie* (Marie's father) reverses neatly to *Le maire de Paris* (the mayor of Paris). *Je vous en prie* (please) becomes *Je vous y prends* (loosely translated: "Gotcha!").

As you might expect of the French, *contrepèterie* often displays a sexual side. For instance:

Le monde comique (humorous world) becomes, less innocently, *le con de Monique* (her, er, sexual organ). *Une pierre fine* (a fine jewel) metamorphoses into *une fière pine* (a proud penis). *Méfiez vous des dons coûteux* (Beware of expensive gifts) becomes *Méfiez vous des cons douteux* (Beware of suspicious vaginas).

Here are some other illustrations of erotic Gallic spooneristic humor:

Il faut être peu pour bien dîner (It costs little to dine well) reverses to *Il faut être deux pour bien piner* (It takes two to have good sex).

Les Anglaises aiment le tennis en pension (English girls at boarding schools like tennis) becomes *Les Anglaises aiment le penis en tension* (English girls are fond of erect penises).

Elle a déjà le choix dans la date (She's already made up her mind about her date) transforms into *Elle a déjà le doigt dans la chatte* (She already has her finger in her—well, you can guess the rest). Note that the two colloquial terms parallel American slang.

Contrepèterie go back to the twelfth century, so the French can boast an even longer and more glorious spooneristic history than we can.

Rabelais is regarded as the father of the form. He also established the explicit content (the term *Rabelaisian* means "broad, coarse humor") that has become its distinctive element.

An often cited Rabelaisian *contrepet* from 1533: *"Femme folle à la Messe/Femme molle à la fesse."* (The woman is crazy in church/she has a soft ass.) Another, equally well known: *"A Beaumont le Vicomte/A beau con le vit monte."* (Gulp! This is much too graphic to translate!)

It's been suggested that, because of its vocabulary and structure, French offers many more opportunities for punnery than other languages. The proliferation of *contrepèterie*, only hinted at in the brief sampling above, lends ample support to that theory.

In German, *Schüttelreim* ("shaking rhyme") is a traditional literary form. Like some of the English-language poems in Chapter 8, these verses are composed in couplets, with the phonemic reversal rhyming with the original word or words.

In his *Jokes and Their Relation to the Unconscious*, Freud quotes this *Schüttelreim*:

Und weil er Geld in Menge hatte
Lag stets er in der Hängematte.

Translation: "And because he had a lot of money, he always lay in a hammock."

Here are a few others, along with idiomatic renderings into English:

Ich wünsche, dass mein Hünengrab
Ich später mal im Grünen hab'.

"I would like to be buried out in the countryside . . . but not for a while!"

Sie fühlen sich mit sechzehn Lenzen gross.
Ist nicht ihr Selbstvertrauen grenzenlos?

"When they are sixteen, they already feel grown up. Isn't their self-confidence limitless?"

Was sagst du zu der Reisewut?
Es rast der Narr. Der Weise ruht.

"What can you say about the passion for travel? Fools rush about frantically, but smart people take it easy."

Transposition puns even occur in Esperanto, where they are called *sonalterno*.

E. James Lieberman, a Washington psychiatrist, is president of the Esperantic Studies Foundation. For a talk about the challenge psychiatry poses to religion, Dr. Lieberman gave his presentation the subtitle *"De Pia Tero al Terapia"* ("From Earthly Piety to Therapy").

Latin can spoonerize too, as shown by this gloomy example: "Canescunt vani/Vanescunt cani" ("The vain turn gray/The gray vanish"). No wonder it's called a dead language!

Now, how about *inadvertent* transpositions? Do people who speak languages other than English ever commit spoonerisms?

Yes, indeed. Accidental reversals occur in a variety of languages, including French, German, Dutch, Welsh, Finnish, Arabic, Croatian, Greek, Burmese, Latin (for those who still speak it), and even American Sign Language!

But the existence of transpositions (whether accidental or deliberate) is contingent upon the nature and structure of the language. In some languages (such as Russian), they are possible but rare, while others (including Chinese and Japanese) employ grammatical structures that make the phenomenon unlikely or impossible.

That's a shame. The speakers of those languages miss out on all the fun!

CHAPTER
10
Here's Champagne to
Real Friends, and . . .

The Wisdom of Spoonerisms

Call it chance, coincidence, or fate, but transpositions sometimes display remarkable profundity and substance.

They can disclose a previously unrecognized truth, cast a new light on an old assumption, or make a critical observation in a barbed and witty manner.

For these most rarefied examples of the art, Richard Lederer shrewdly suggests the term *forkerism*: "A spoonerism with a point."

The chiastic form (literary reversal or inversion) has long been recognized by playwrights, politicians, and speechwriters as a powerful rhetorical device. Because it resonates emotionally, it has been used to good effect in the Bible, by Shakespeare, and by U.S. Presidents, among others.

Some famous examples:

"Many that are first shall be last; and the last shall be first." "Better a witty fool than a foolish wit." "When the going gets tough, the tough get going." "Some eat to live; some live to eat." "People don't plan to fail; they fail to plan." "Let us never negotiate out of fear, but let us never fear to negotiate." "Ask not what your country can do for you . . ." And so on.

But this potent technique should by no means be relegated to history.

After all, we live at the dawning of an age—or perhaps it's the aging of a dawn. As it is truly said by the Yale crew team: Ye shall seep what ye row.

Consider then the wisdom of the following:

Alcoholism: The wrath of grapes.
  —Selma Glasser, Johnny Hart ("The Wizard
    of Id"), a *New York Times* editorialist . . . and
    lots of other witty people

The hand that cradles the rock must not rule this world.
  —Larry T. McGehee, former chancellor,
    University of Tennessee at Martin, in a
    commencement address at the University of
    Alabama, Tuscaloosa (also, somewhat
    differently, S. J. Perelman)

Religious traditionalists on more liberal ministries:
Paul is appealing, but Peale is appalling.
                    —Inspired by a campaign remark
                      by Adlai Stevenson

Margaret Thatcher's revolutionary transformation
of England's economy: Britannia waives the rules.
                —Probably many independent creators,
                  including Leslie Bricusse in a lyric in
                  the 1963 musical *Pickwick*

Neville Chamberlain: He took his countries in the weekend.

—William F. Buckley, Jr.

On the agonies of lyric writing: The road to all these good intentions is paved with hell.

—Alan Jay Lerner

Put not your trust in money, but put your money in trust.

—Oliver Wendell Holmes

Despite assiduous research, I have been unable to identify the originators of the next six specimens, which must perforce be credited as "Source Unknown":

The feminist movement's clarion to homemakers: Don't iron while the strike is hot.

Productivity crisis in academia: The leisure of the theory class.

I'd rather have a bottle in front of me than a frontal lobotomy.

Sage counsel from Planned Parenthood: Accidents cause people.

If you don't have what it takes, they'll take what you have.

Dialogue of a long-married couple: "You were more gallant when you were a boy." "You were more buoyant when you were a gal."

And now what may be the single most perfect transposition pun of all:

Time wounds all heels.

It has been attributed to Groucho Marx and radio writer-performer Jane Ace. Thousands of other people probably assume they thought of it first.

That aphorism strikes an appropriate chord on which to conclude this volume, along with the following toast (of unknown origin, but quoted by John Skow):

> Here's champagne to real friends . . .
> and real pain to sham friends.

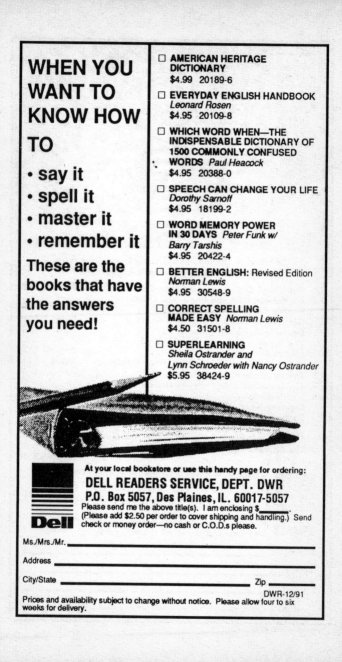